The Euthanasia Debate

D1331054

ISSUES

(formerly Issues for the Nineties)

Volume 4

Editor

Craig Donnellan

Independence

Educational Publishers

Cambridge

First published by Independence
PO Box 295
Cambridge CB1 3XP
England

British Library Cataloguing in Publication Data
The Euthanasia Debate – (Issues Series)
I. Donnellan, Craig II. Series
179.7

ISBN 1 86168 090 2   418786
N179.7

Printed in Great Britain
The Burlington Press
Cambridge

Typeset by
Claire Boyd

Cover
The illustration on the front cover is by
Katherine Fleming.

CONTENTS

Introduction

The Euthanasia Debate is the fourth volume in the series: **Issues**. The aim of this series is to offer up-to-date information about important issues in our world.

The Euthanasia Debate looks at the moral, social and medical aspects of euthanasia.

The information comes from a wide variety of sources and includes:
Government reports and statistics
Newspaper reports and features
Magazine articles and surveys
Literature from lobby groups
and charitable organisations.

It is hoped that, as you read about the many aspects of the issues explored in this book, you will critically evaluate the information presented. It is important that you decide whether you are being presented with facts or opinions. Does the writer give a biased or an unbiased report? If an opinion is being expressed, do you agree with the writer?

The Euthanasia Debate offers a useful starting-point for those who need convenient access to information about the many issues involved. However, it is only a starting-point. At the back of the book is a list of organisations which you may want to contact for further information.

*****

Frequently asked questions

Information from the Voluntary Euthanasia Society of Scotland (VESS)

What is voluntary euthanasia?

When we hear the phrase 'voluntary euthanasia' people generally think of one of two things: the active termination of life at the patient's request as it occurs in the Netherlands (or similar proposals in other countries); or the Nazi extermination programme of murder. Many people have beliefs about whether euthanasia is right or wrong, often without being able to define it clearly. Some people take an extreme view, while many fall somewhere between the two camps. Dictionary definitions avail us little, as there will always be large groups of people that claim it means something else. The apparent derivation 'a gentle and easy death' (from the Greek, *eu thanatos*) hardly describes what we mean. Even extending the definition to include 'bringing about of this, especially in the case of incurable and painful disease' (*Oxford English Dictionary*) hardly covers it – hospices often succeed in bringing about a peaceful death, but they don't perform euthanasia!

VESS

In the Netherlands, the only country where euthanasia is openly practised, euthanasia is defined as 'the intentional termination of life by another at the explicit request of the person who dies' (Netherlands State Commission on Euthanasia). The argument then often centres on the voluntariness of the request. How can one be sure that it is voluntary? Supporters of the voluntary euthanasia movement generally believe that it would be possible to devise sufficient safeguards to ensure that the request was voluntary and that people could never feel pressured.

The Dutch are critical of their own system and are continually refining and testing it – though generally they feel that it respects human rights and is part of good medicine. They get rid of the word 'voluntary' since the 'explicit request' is part of their definition of euthanasia.

An explicit request is objectively observable, whereas voluntariness depends somewhat on interpretation. Some opponents of euthanasia suggest that the true will is impaired if one is asking to die and that therefore there is no voluntariness. Most people would agree if the person was emotionally distraught over, say, being jilted by a lover, or if the person was psychiatrically of unsound mind, but most of us view more considered statements as voluntary, especially if we are unable to find any evidence to the contrary.

Obviously the Dutch definition needs careful implementation to ensure voluntariness, and the Dutch attempt to do this by a series of safeguards within a close doctor-patient relationship, a high standard and availability of palliative care, and general public support. There is much debate over whether we could have a similar system in, say, Britain, but we feel that the present system is unsatisfactory and so we press for reform.

One of the few certainties of life is death, but in the twentieth century it is still a taboo subject. The 'forbidden' nature of death adds to the unnamed fears and worries that most people feel when asked to confront the idea of their own death. Yet once people can overcome their reluctance to discuss the subject,

most often what is revealed is not the fear of death itself, but the manner of dying. The difficulty of thinking about 'death with dignity' is that it implies that one day you, or someone you love, may be in a position to want that choice.

No one can prevent death finally, but we can and should ensure that the dying process is a gentle and peaceful one. When life consists of a few agonising, drugged weeks, many patients beg their doctors to help them die, and many doctors, mindful of the ethics of their profession, feel forced to refuse. Those who, out of compassion, accede to such a request, know they are breaking the law and putting their careers at risk.

This is the dilemma which faces all of us now. Should we, as potential patients, have the legal right to ask our doctors to help us die when the end of life is in sight and our suffering severe?

Why the need for societies?

In England, the Voluntary Euthanasia Society was founded in 1935 by the late Dr C. Killick Millard MD, DSc. Its principal object was to make it legal for an adult person, who is suffering severe distress from an incurable illness, to receive medical help to die at their own considered request.

In 1980 Scottish Exit (now the Voluntary Euthanasia Society of Scotland or VESS) became an independent group, and published *How to Die With Dignity*. This booklet, by Dr George Mair, was the first guide to self-deliverance in the world. An updated version, together with the well-researched modern supplement *Departing Drugs*, is still available to members of at least three months' standing, as long as they specifically request it. Members can receive the booklet in Scotland, England or anywhere in the world. VESS also acts as a centre and focus for research concerning medical decisions at the end of life, and particularly living wills. The *VESS Newsletter* is considered a leading source of information. VESS can provide information and support to members of the public, doctors, lawyers, educational institutions and students, politicians and the media.

Individuals should note, however, that while seeking a change of the law, we will only act within the law as it stands

The history of reform shows that humane and well-argued proposals only tend to pass into law when there is a strong public voice behind them. The people who struggle against inhumanity make their mark by creating a better world. We can't help those who have died in abject suffering, but we can work for the good of those whose death is yet to come – not only by striving for better, caring services, but by restoring control to the individual who has entered the last phase of life.

Is there growing support for the movement?

A National Opinion Poll, in April 1993, showed that 81% of Scots agree with our aims for a change in the law. A phone-in after a TV programme gave a figure of 93% in agreement, from a total of 23,000 calls. A survey published in the *British Medical Journal* in 1994 showed that a considerable number of doctors are already acceding to requests for active voluntary euthanasia. Many more doctors feel that a change in the law is overdue. Yet any move towards legislation of voluntary euthanasia has so far been blocked by opponents.

Opposing voices tend to reveal an ignorance of the true nature of voluntary euthanasia. Misunderstandings abound, and we hope in this information to lift and remove any fears and misapprehensions. If you wish to write or phone, we are also glad to answer any queries.

International support is growing rapidly. A number of countries are actively considering legislative reform. Right-to-die societies around the world have increasing support from the swiftly growing numbers of individuals demanding their rights to self-determination.

Does the society encourage euthanasia for the old and infirm?

There can be no voluntary 'euthanasia' if any persuasion is present. In all humane societies there is proper provision for caring for the elderly and infirm. Such facilities are also paid for out of taxes in a normal working life, and an individual has a right to choose to benefit from these services – the individual has the right to choose the type of care he or she would like, or to decline further treatment. No one should be driven to contemplate suicide through lack of service, care or support.

While it is often the old and infirm who choose self-deliverance, the choice has been made in the light of each individual's quality of life.

Love of life is a primitive instinct: no one should be persuaded to die through propaganda. But a conviction, deeply held for whatever reason, that the time has come, should be respected, and everyone should have the right to choose release.

I want to die. Please can the society help me?

VESS is not a suicide club. As a pressure group we seek to bring about a change in the law, but we must act, and be seen to be acting, within the law. Neither do we encourage suicide stemming from irrational or emotional impulses. Although we have no formal association with the Samaritans, we urge any emotionally traumatised individual contemplating suicide to get in touch with them. We also stress the importance of clear and full diagnosis of existing conditions if a person is already ill.

What does VESS feel about malformed babies, the mentally handicapped or the incurably insane?

VESS seeks only the legislation of voluntary euthanasia. Handicapped babies and the mentally retarded cannot make that voluntary decision, and so are not included in our remit. VESS also presses equally strongly for safeguards against any type of so-called euthanasia that does not stem from a clear, well-informed and voluntary request on the part of the individual. We stand for freedom of choice, and this also includes that of

individuals and doctors who are opposed to our views but do not seek to impose those views on others.

Why do you need voluntary euthanasia when there is the hospice movement?

There have been enormous advances in the care of the terminally ill, and for many, the lucky ones who find a place in a hospice, this has proved adequate to ensure that they come to a peaceful and dignified end.

Unfortunately, even with medical advances and excellent hospice research in palliative care, severe indignity, pain and distress cannot always be controlled. The hospices' most optimistic estimate for pain control is 95%. In practice, in ordinary hospitals, it may be as low as 30%.

There are conditions such as cancer, strokes, acute arthritis, and more recently AIDS, to name just a few, where all the medical skills in the world aren't enough for a particular individual case. If that person, after undergoing all possible treatment, still feels enough is enough, they should have the right to be helped to die.

The phrase 'terminal illness' suggests a way of looking at death, not as the moment of brain death, but as a process lasting some period of time; once this more realistic view is embraced, and the fact of dying accepted by the individual, the doctors and the relatives, what can be gained by ensuring that the process of dying is prolonged as much as possible? Now, a dying person's wishes often count as nothing: hence we want a change in the law.

Why isn't the law changed?

Often the medical profession claim there is no need for legislation. In fact, Lord Dawson of Penn, the royal physician, argued that helping patients to die was part of good doctoring. We now know he had practical experience of this, in timing the end of George V. A Bill promoted in 1936, seeking to permit voluntary euthanasia in certain circumstances and with certain safeguards, was rejected, but public sympathy was with it. Subsequent attempts to reform the law have met with similar fates, including in 1990 an Early Day Motion on the subject of voluntary euthanasia, and a 1993 Select Committee of the House of Lords.

By mobilising public concern this could be changed. You can help by supporting us; you could write to your MP, or open a debate in your newspaper.

But surely suicide isn't illegal?

Suicide has long been legal in Scotland and, since 1961, in the rest of Britain. However, aiding another person towards his or her own suicide is still illegal, no matter how laudable the motives. It is this situation which makes it impossible for doctors to practise active euthanasia.

There is the added difficulty that by the time many people are driven to contemplate suicide because of their suffering, they are not physically able to accomplish the act. The law is inconsistent inasmuch as it tolerates suicide, but outlaws the means. To deny a person control over his or her own life is immoral. It is an abuse of human rights, and should be illegal.

© 1999 Chris Docker

I HAVE A TERMINAL DISEASE...

I'm IN CONSTANT PAIN, I CAN'T DO ANYTHING...

MY BODILY FUNCTIONS ARE BREAKING DOWN...

I—

GEE - YOU'RE NOT IN A FIT STATE TO MAKE ANY LIFE OR DEATH DECISIONS!

SIMON KNEEBONE

Answers to frequently asked questions

Information from the International Anti-Euthanasia Task Force

Euthanasia is one of the most important public policy issues being debated today. The outcome of that debate will profoundly affect family relationships, interaction between doctors and patients, and concepts of basic morality. With so much at stake, more is needed than a duel of one-liners, slogans and sound bites.

The following answers to frequently asked questions are designed as starting-points for considering the issues. For more detailed information see the documented, in-depth material available at our web site.

What is euthanasia?

Answer: Formerly called 'mercy killing', euthanasia means intentionally making someone die, rather than allowing that person to die naturally.

Put bluntly, euthanasia means killing in the name of compassion.

What is the difference between euthanasia and assisted suicide?

Answer: In euthanasia, one person does something that directly kills another. For example, a doctor gives a lethal injection to a patient.

In assisted suicide, a non-suicidal person knowingly and intentionally provides the means or acts in some way to help a suicidal person kill himself or herself. For example, a doctor writes a prescription for poison, or someone hooks up a face mask and tubing to a canister of carbon monoxide and then instructs the suicidal person on how to push a lever so that she'll be gassed to death.

For all practical purposes, any distinction between euthanasia and assisted suicide has been abandoned today. Information contained in these answers to frequently asked questions will use the word 'euthanasia' for both euthanasia and assisted suicide.

Doesn't euthanasia insure a dignified death?

Answer: 'Death with dignity' has become a catch phrase used by euthanasia activists, but there's nothing dignified about the methods they advocate. For example, one euthanasia organisation distributes a pamphlet on how to cause suffocation with a plastic bag. Most of Jack Kevorkian's 'subjects', as he calls them, have been gassed to death with carbon monoxide and some have had their bodies dumped in vehicles left in parking lots.

With legalised euthanasia, wouldn't patients die peacefully, surrounded by their families and doctors, instead of being suffocated by plastic bags or gassed with carbon monoxide as happens now?

Answer: No. Campaigners for euthanasia often say that, but it's not true.

In the two places where laws were passed to allow euthanasia, it was clear that legalising euthanasia only legitimised the use of plastic bags and carbon monoxide to kill vulnerable people.

For example, immediately following the passage of Oregon's Measure 16, those who had said that it would enable people to die peacefully with pills did an immediate about face and admitted that it would permit the types of activities carried out by Jack Kevorkian. They also said that, if pills were used, a plastic bag should also be used to ensure death.

A similar situation occurred in Australia's Northern Territory where proponents of euthanasia painted pictures of a calm, peaceful death with the patient surrounded by loved ones.

When guidelines for the Australian measure (which has now been repealed) were written after its passage, it was acknowledged that carbon monoxide gas would be permitted. It was recommended that, if drugs were used for the euthanasia death, family members should be warned that they may wish to leave the room when the patient is being killed since the death may be very unpleasant to observe. (Lethal injections often cause violent convulsions and muscle spasms.)

A particularly chilling method of ending a patient's life was proposed by Dr. Philip Nitschke, a leading Australian euthanasia activist, when he announced that he had developed a computer program for euthanasia so that doctors could remove themselves from the actual death scene.

Doesn't modern technology keep people alive who would have died in the past?

Answer: Modern medicine has definitely lengthened life spans. In the early part of this century, pneumonia, appendicitis, diabetes, high blood pressure – even an abscessed tooth – likely meant death, often accompanied by excruciating pain. Women had shorter life expectancies than men since many died in childbirth. Antibiotics, immunisations, surgery and many of today's routine therapies or medications were unknown then.

A lot of people think that the person whose death would be a result of euthanasia or assisted suicide would be someone who doesn't want to be forced to remain alive by being hooked up to machines. But the law already permits patients or their surrogates to direct that such interventions be withheld or withdrawn.

Should people be forced to stay alive?

Answer: No. And neither the law nor medical ethics requires that 'everything be done' to keep a person alive. Insistence, against the patient's wishes, that death be postponed by every means available is contrary to law and practice. It would also be cruel and inhumane.

There comes a time when continued attempts to cure are not compassionate, wise, or medically sound. That's where hospice, including in-home hospice care, can be of such help.

That is the time when all efforts should be placed on making the patient's remaining time comfortable. Then, all interventions should be directed to alleviating pain and other symptoms as well as to the provision of emotional and spiritual support for both the patient and the patient's loved ones.

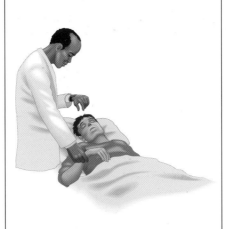

Does the government have the right to make people suffer?

Answer: Absolutely not. Likewise, the government should not have the right to give one group of people (e.g. doctors) the right to kill another group of people (e.g. their patients).

Euthanasia activists often claim that laws against euthanasia are government-mandated suffering. But this claim would be similar to saying that laws against selling contaminated food are government-mandated starvation.

Laws against euthanasia are in place to prevent abuse and to protect people from unscrupulous doctors and others. They are not, and never have been, intended to make anyone suffer.

But shouldn't people have the right to commit suicide?

Answer: People do have the power to commit suicide. Suicide and attempted suicide are not criminalised. Each and every year, in the United States alone, there are more suicides than homicides.

Suicide is a tragic, individual act. Euthanasia is not about a private act. It's about letting one person facilitate the death of another. That is a matter of very public concern since it can lead to tremendous abuse, exploitation and erosion of care for the most vulnerable people among us.

Euthanasia is not about giving rights to the person who dies but, instead, is about changing the law and public policy so that doctors, relatives and others can directly and intentionally end another person's life.

This change would not give rights to the person who is killed, but to the person who does the killing. In other words, euthanasia is not about the right to die. It's about the right to kill.

Isn't 'kill' too strong a word for euthanasia?

Answer: No. The word 'kill' means 'to cause the death of'.

In 1989, a group of physicians published a report in the *New England Journal of Medicine* in which they concluded that it would be morally acceptable for doctors to give patients suicide information and a prescription for deadly drugs so they can kill themselves. Dr Ronald Cranford, one of the authors of the report, publicly acknowledged that this is 'the same as killing the patient'.

While changes in the law would lead to euthanasia being considered a 'medical intervention', the reality would not change – the patient would be killed.

Proponents of euthanasia often use euphemisms like 'deliverance', 'aid-in-dying' and 'gentle landing'. If a public policy has to be promoted with euphemisms, that may be because the use of accurate, descriptive language would demonstrate that the policy is misguided.

Wouldn't euthanasia only be available to people who are terminally ill?

Answer: Absolutely not. There are two problems here – the definition of 'terminal' and the changes that have already taken place to extend euthanasia to those who aren't 'terminally ill'.

There are many definitions for the word 'terminal'. For example, when he spoke to the National Press Club in 1992, Jack Kevorkian said that a terminal illness was 'any disease that curtails life even for a day'. The co-founder of the Hemlock Society often refers to 'terminal old age'. Some laws define 'terminal' condition as one from which death will occur in a 'relatively short time'. Others state that 'terminal' means that death is expected within six months or less.

Even where a specific life expectancy (like six months) is

referred to, medical experts acknowledge that it is virtually impossible to predict the life expectancy of a particular patient. Moreover, some people diagnosed as terminally ill don't die for years, if at all, from the diagnosed condition.

Increasingly, however, euthanasia activists have dropped references to terminal illness, replacing them with such phrases as 'hopelessly ill', 'desperately ill', 'incurably ill', 'hopeless condition', and 'meaningless life.'

An article in the journal *Suicide and Life-Threatening Behavior* described assisted suicide guidelines for those with a hopeless condition. 'Hopeless condition' was defined to include terminal illness, severe physical or psychological pain, physical or mental debilitation or deterioration, or a quality of life that is no longer acceptable to the individual. That means just about anybody who has a suicidal impulse .

In a May 1996 speech to the prestigious American Psychiatric Association, George Delury (who assisted in the 1995 death of his wife who had multiple sclerosis) suggested that 'hopelessly ill people or people past age sixty just apply for a licence to die' and that such a licence should be granted without examination by doctors.

Wouldn't euthanasia only be at a patient's request?

Answer: No. As one of their major arguments, euthanasia proponents claim that euthanasia should be considered 'medical treatment'. If one accepts the notion that euthanasia is good, then it would not only be inappropriate, but discriminatory, to deny this 'good' to a person solely on the basis of that person's being too young or too mentally incapacitated to make the request.

In fact, a surrogate's decision is often treated, for legal purposes, as if it had been made by the patient. That means children and people who can't make their own decisions could well be euthanised.

Suppose, however, that surrogates were not permitted to choose death for another. The problem of how free a death request would be still remains.

If euthanasia becomes accepted in policy or in practice, subtle, even unintended, coercion will be unavoidable.

If death is inevitable, shouldn't a person who is dying and wants to commit suicide have the right to do so?

Answer: It's really important to understand that suicide in a person who has been diagnosed with a terminal illness is no different than suicide for someone who is not considered terminally ill. Depression, family conflict, feelings of abandonment, hopelessness, etc. lead to suicide – regardless of one's physical condition.

Studies have shown that if pain and depression are adequately treated in a dying person – as they would be in a suicidal non-dying person – the desire to commit suicide evaporates.

Suicide among the terminally ill, like suicide among the population in general, is a tragic event that cuts short the life of the victim and leaves devastated survivors.

Certainly no one would be forced into euthanasia, would they?

Answer: Physical force is highly unlikely. But emotional and psychological pressures could become overpowering for depressed or dependent people. If the choice of euthanasia is considered as good as a decision to receive care, many people will feel guilty for not choosing death.

Financial considerations, added to the concern about 'being a burden', could serve as powerful forces that would lead a person to 'choose' euthanasia or assisted suicide.

Even the smallest gesture could create a gentle nudge into the grave. Such was evidenced in greeting cards sold at the 1991 national conference of the Hemlock Society.

According to the conference programme, the cards were designed to be given to those who are terminally ill. One card in particular exemplified the core of the movement that would remove the last shred of hope remaining to a person faced with a life-threatening illness. It carried the message, 'I learned you'll be leaving us soon.'

Isn't euthanasia sometimes the only way to relieve excruciating pain?

Answer: Quite the contrary. Euthanasia activists exploit the natural fear people have of suffering and dying, and often imply that when cure is no longer likely, there are only two alternatives: euthanasia or unbearable pain.

For example, an official of Choice in Dying, a right-to-die organisation, said refusing to permit euthanasia 'would, in fact, be to abandon the patient to a horrifying death'.

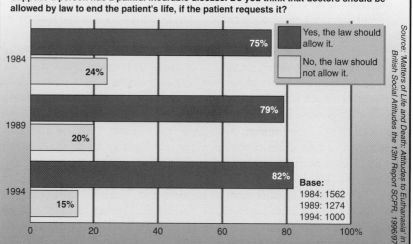

Public attitudes to voluntary euthanasia

The graph below shows that, in 1994, 82% of respondents answered in the affirmative when asked if a doctor should terminate the life of a terminally ill patient who expressed the wish to die. In studies other than the one cited, the percentage of people polled who agreed with voluntary euthanasia is lower, but these studies still document majority support for it.

Suppose a person has a painful incurable disease. Do you think that doctors should be allowed by law to end the patient's life, if the patient requests it?

Yes, the law should allow it.
No, the law should not allow it.

1984: 75% / 24%
1989: 79% / 20%
1994: 82% / 15%

Base:
1984: 1562
1989: 1274
1994: 1000

Source: *Matters of Life and Death: Attitudes to Euthanasia* in *British Social Attitudes the 13th Report SCPR, 1996/97*

Such an irresponsible statement fails to note that virtually all pain can be eliminated and that – in those rare cases where it can't be eliminated – it can still be reduced significantly if proper treatment is provided.

It is a national and international scandal that so many people do not get adequate pain control. But killing is not the answer to that scandal. The solution is to mandate better education of health care professionals on these crucial issues, to expand access to health care, and to inform patients about their rights as consumers.

Everyone – whether it be a person with a life-threatening illness or a chronic condition – has the right to pain relief. With modern advances in pain control, no patient should ever be in excruciating pain. However, most doctors have never had a course in pain management so they're unaware of what to do.

If a patient who is under a doctor's care is in excruciating pain, there's definitely a need to find a different doctor. But that doctor should be one who will control the pain, not one who will kill the patient.

There are board-certified specialists in pain management who will not only help alleviate physical pain but are skilled in providing necessary support to deal with emotional suffering and depression that often accompanies physical pain.

Isn't opposition to euthanasia just an attempt to impose religious beliefs on others?

Answer: No. Euthanasia leaders have attempted for a long time to make it seem that anyone against euthanasia is trying to impose his or her own religion on society. But that's not the case.

People on both sides of the euthanasia controversy claim membership in religious denominations. There are also individuals on both sides who claim no religious affiliation at all. But it's even more important to realise that this is not a religious debate. It's a debate about public policy and the law.

The fact that the religious

convictions of some people parallel what has been long-standing public policy does not disqualify them from taking a stand on an issue.

For example, there are laws that prohibit sales clerks from stealing company profits. Although these laws coincide with religious beliefs, it would be absurd to suggest that such laws should be eliminated. And it would be equally ridiculous to say that a person who has religious opposition to stealing shouldn't be able to support laws against stealing.

Likewise, the fact that the religious convictions of some euthanasia opponents parallel what has been long-standing public policy does not disqualify them from taking a stand on the issue.

Throughout all of modern history, laws have prohibited mercy killing. The need for such laws has been, and should continue to be, debated on the basis of public policy, and people of any or no religious belief should have the right to be involved in that debate.

In Washington state, where an attempt to legalise euthanasia and assisted suicide failed in 1991, polls taken within days of the vote indicated that fewer than ten per cent of those who opposed the measure had done so for religious reasons.

The following year, voters in California turned down a similar proposal. During the campaign, euthanasia leaders claimed that all opposition was religious, yet the

groups opposing the measure that would have legalised euthanasia and assisted suicide included the California Commission on Ageing, California Medical Association, California Nurses Association, California Psychiatric Association and the California State Hospice Association. In addition, all major newspapers throughout the state, including the *Los Angeles Times*, *San Francisco Chronicle*, and *San Diego Union Tribune* took strong editorial positions against the measure.

Where is euthanasia legal?

Answer: At the present time, the State of Oregon has the world's only law specifically permitting a doctor to prescribe lethal drugs for the purpose of ending a patient's life.

Although euthanasia is widely practised in the Netherlands, it remains technically illegal.

In 1995 Australia's Northern Territory approved a euthanasia bill. It went into effect in 1996 and was overturned by the Australian Parliament in 1997.

For the latest about euthanasia developments throughout the world, see the *IAETF Update*.

• The above is an extract from the International Anti-Euthanasia Task Force (IAETF) web site which can be found on http://www.iaetf.org Their address is: PO Box 760, Steubenville, OH 43952, 740-282-3810. USA

© International Anti-Euthanasia Task Force (IAETF), 1998

Killing for mercy?

Information from Christian Action Research and Education (CARE)

Dr Christian Barnard of South Africa described how he decided one night to end his patient's life. She had a growth in her womb and was writhing and screaming with the pain. He assumed she was dying. He went out for the morphine and returned only to find her sound asleep. He decided to wait till morning before giving her the injection. When he awoke, the woman was serene, in her right mind, and almost pain free. Six weeks later, she left the clinic.

Euthanasia

From the Greek word to 'die well'. Literally, 'a good death'. In everyday speech, it describes the act of killing a person who is suffering from a distressing mental or physical condition.

'Whenever euthanasia is proposed the supposed beneficiaries are always cited as being those with incurable conditions. I fall into this category having been born with spina bifida. In a death on demand culture, if I were to express suicidal thoughts, I would probably be taken at my word, whereas a similarly depressed able bodied person would not. Thus the decisive factor would not be the wish to die, but the physical condition of the person making the request.' Alison Davis (*Daily Telegraph* 5/90)

Mercy killing

Another term for euthanasia. Killing, allegedly on grounds of 'mercy'.

Professor Duncan Vere tells the story of a patient who begged to be 'put to death'. The professor gave him a drug and for a few hours the man thought he was dead. When he awoke the next day however, he had forgotten about the whole episode!

What is euthanasia?

One of the biggest problems in discussing the rights and wrongs of euthanasia is that people use the word to mean different things. For some of us, euthanasia conjures up pictures of granny snuggling under the duvet as her doctor mixes the fatal potion at her bedside. Others might associate it with the decision to turn off the life-support machine attached to an unconscious road accident victim. Yet for others euthanasia will bring to mind something more personal – we may be reminded of a friend or relative who died in what seemed like unnecessary pain. Could 'euthanasia' have been an option there? A lot depends on what we mean by the word 'euthanasia'. Because unless we know what we're talking about, we won't be able to decide whether it is right or wrong. And the best place to start is to find out what euthanasia is not!

What euthanasia is not

In the examples that follow we can see that the doctor has no intention of killing his patient – that is why they do not count as 'euthanasia'.

Stopping treatment

If a person is near death, a doctor may decide to stop life-prolonging treatment. This may be because the drugs and treatment are no longer giving effect or because their side-effects are causing the patient a lot of distress for very little gain. This is not euthanasia. Doctors should be able to recognise when a person is dying and should do all they can to help the patient die in peace. Consider the following, story: 'When I was a young doctor, I remember looking after a man whose lungs were seriously damaged by a particular disease for which there was no cure. He came into hospital in the last stages of respiratory failure. I wanted to rush in with machines and drugs to save him. But the wise physician for whom I was working said "Enough is enough". Then I realised, my duty was plain – it was to relieve the patient's distress and see that he died in dignity and comfort.'

Switching off a respirator

After severe injury, many patients are put on a respirator – equipment to help them breathe whilst doctors assess the degree of injury. Where death has occurred, the life-support machine is turned off. This is not euthanasia since the doctor has not intentionally ended their patient's life.

Treating pain

To treat pain in dying patients, doctors have to give large doses of strong drugs at frequent intervals. Sometimes it looks as if the person is made worse by the drug rather than better, and they may even die! This

is not euthanasia. All drugs have side-effects. And the side-effect of controlling pain may be to weaken the patient and bring death more quickly. For example, someone with a weak heart may find breathing painful and the doctor may decide to give a dose of morphine to relieve the patient's distress. However, the morphine will also make the patient's breathing less efficient – and so raise the chances that the patient will die sooner than expected!

What euthanasia is

Euthanasia is defined by intent. Where a doctor, friend or relative intentionally ends a person's life to 'finish their suffering', this is euthanasia. In Holland (where euthanasia is permitted though not legalised), there are many such cases. In 1987, the *Sunday Times* produced a long feature on one Dutch doctor who has killed many of his patients over the past 10 years. It describes how, at the patient's request, he killed them using an injection or a drip of poisonous drugs.

What's all the fuss about?

First, we must look at what the pro-euthanasiasts want.

- They want to make an exception to the present law so that killing for the sake of mercy is not a punishable offence.
- They want patients to have the legal right to demand that a doctor kill them.
- They want doctors to be able to kill patients without fear of punishment.
- They want people to be encouraged to declare in advance what sort of treatment they should or should not receive if they become incapacitated through accident or illness. These 'declarations' are known as 'living wills' and would have legally binding status (as they do in many US States).

What's wrong with mercy killing?

Demands like these raise many serious problems

- Doctors make mistakes. Much of the pro-euthanasia argument depends on the naive assumption that doctors have the ability to know precisely if and when a patient will die.
- 'A woman of 86 recovered yesterday from an "irreversible" coma and began talking and eating on her own. Dr Michael Wolff, a specialist in geriatric medicine, told last Friday's court hearing there was no chance Mrs Coons would recover. He said he was at a loss to explain what had happened.' (*Daily Telegraph* 4/89).
- Psychological and emotional pressures. When a sick or elderly person asks for euthanasia, how can we be sure they are making a free choice to die? How can we be sure it is their decision and that no one has pressurised them into it? We all know how many old people are afraid of 'being a burden' to their children and grandchildren. Subtle pressure from the family – even things like lack of living space – may push an old person into asking for euthanasia if it were available.
- Euthanasia is not simply a personal affair as some would have us believe. It is about one person agreeing with another person that their life is no longer worth living. Clearly, any doctor who thought that his patient's life was worth living wouldn't perform euthanasia! If this change were incorporated in law, this would be a radical threat to all of us. We would no longer be protected from attack because we are human beings but because certain other members of society think we have worthwhile lives. The danger for those who may not be considered to have worthwhile lives – the elderly, the handicapped, psychiatric patients, long-term prisoners – is all too clear. The logic of voluntary euthanasia is involuntary euthanasia.
- A damaged medical profession. A good relationship between patient and doctor has to be based on trust. If we knew that our doctor had killed as well as cured other patients in the past, would we really trust our doctor with all our hang-ups and fears? One survey in Holland (where euthanasia is practised openly) showed that 63% of people in old age homes feared that one day their lives might be ended without their consent or knowledge.
- Loose terminology – unforeseen results. We all know the problems of signing legal documents! You need a lawyer just to explain them first! Imagine the dangers of a form in which you give someone the right to end your life under certain circumstances! These forms – called living wills – are becoming increasingly popular in the USA. However, evidence suggests that the people who sign them have little idea of how they may be interpreted by doctors at a future date. There are no grounds for giving doctors powers to end life – especially when the forms are open to widely differing interpretations.
- Giving doctors too much power. Doctors themselves would be the first to admit that they are in positions of great power over their patients, the 'doctor knows best' syndrome. To add to what some already see as an unhealthy patient-doctor power balance by giving the doctor even more power – the power to kill – is a very unsafe and unwise thing to do.
- Doctors have always said 'No!' For thousands of years, doctors have refused to aid suicide or participate in euthanasia. Their job was not to kill, but to cure. Recently the medical profession published a report on euthanasia (*BMA Report* 1988) in which it restated its opposition to any moves to change the law: 'We do not, at present, see that any general policy condoning medical interventions to terminate life can be reconciled with commitments to good medical practice.'
- Missing: chief witness for the prosecution. There are many problems with making an exception to the laws against murder. Such laws are there to show that we respect every human being whatever their state of health and to protect us all from the harmful encroachment of others. If we admit that in some circumstances it is right to legalise the killing of

one private citizen (a patient) by another (a doctor), then where is the protection for the rest of us? If foul play is suspected, proof of wrongdoing will be virtually impossible to obtain since the chief witness is now dead!

- Killing for those who want it – and for those who don't. If we accept euthanasia for those who request it we will soon accept it as necessary for those who haven't requested it. Already some doctors and philosophers are talking about killing handicapped newborn babies. One doctor recently argued that we should allow families to decide whether their elderly parents ought to be killed or not 'for the sake of the survival of the unit'. These ideas are already around. If we legalise euthanasia – we will simply provide a seed bed for these horrendous views to grow.

Christian considerations

The Christian understanding of life also leads right away from euthanasia.

- We are made in the image of God; human life is therefore uniquely precious. Human life is God's gift to us; we are not the owners but rather the stewards of it. We belong to God because God made us.
- The Christian belongs to Christ in a special way because we have been redeemed. Our aim is not to please ourselves but to serve Christ who intercedes on our behalf with a loving Father. Whilst not removing us from the trials and tribulations common to all in this world, he is working things out for the good of all who love him.
- There are many instances of people in Scripture whom we could regard as prime candidates for euthanasia. Yet those who most 'needed' this sort of help were not the ones to take it: Job, David, Jeremiah, Jesus. Only the apostate King Saul saw suicide as a helpful option. When Job's wife told him to 'curse God and die' he knew that she spoke as an unbeliever, someone who did not recognise God as Creator of all things.

The alternatives

- Good medical care. Research has shown that 85% of patients with pain can be totally relieved with the help of drugs; a further 10% can be relieved almost completely; and the remaining 5% can have their pain removed for much of the time. No one need die in pain. Doctors need specialised training in this area to learn how to use drugs in the most efficient way.
- Hospices. Hospices provide a positive homely environment for the seriously ill and dying patient. One woman said 'I came here to die of cancer. Now I have learned how to live with cancer.' Hospices allow people to live to the full right to the end and they are staffed by people who are specially trained in the needs of the dying.
- Company. Some 2.2 million old people live alone in the UK, seldom going out or seeing friends. Loneliness is one of the main causes of depression and illness – one of the main reasons for requesting euthanasia. We must keep in touch with our neighbours and our family; a visit once a week could make a world of difference to someone who may otherwise live and die unnoticed.

Further information

The following are available from CARE:

1. *Living Dangerously – Euthanasia Explained* – £12.99. This video helps to understand the complex contemporary moral issue of euthanasia. Has been used widely in schools, churches, youth and other groups. Comes complete with a workbook. (Reduced price for church leaders and teachers/lecturers £9.99.)

2. *Euthanasia . . . Death on Demand* – £2.00. An eight-page resource that looks at the facts and figures behind the debate on euthanasia and examines what is happening in other countries.

3. *Living Wills – The Issues Examined* – £1.00. This briefing paper examines the biblical, medical and legal arguments about whether or not living wills are in the best interests of patients.

4. *Euthanasia – killing for mercy?* – £2.45. CARE's Information Pack on euthanasia, includes *Living Wills* Briefing Paper, *Euthanasia Death on Demand* Action File and *Euthanasia – Killing for Mercy?* leaflet and other information for individuals or groups who want to study this important topic.

5. *A Time to Die?*, by Wesley McGowan MD – 50p. An excellent booklet which clearly and authoritatively presents the key argments against euthanasia.

6. *Euthanasia: The Heart of the Matter*, by Andrew Dunnett – £6.99. Vital reading for understanding the euthanasia debate. Ten well-respected people who are helping to shape the debate have been interviewed for this book.

- The above is an extract from the CARE web site which can be found at http://www.care.org.uk

Euthanasia – is it right?

Do you believe in playing God? Or should death be a decision that nobody has the right to take? We asked you to tell us . . .

Miranda Peake, 23
Bookshop assistant, London
I think very old people with no quality of life should have the right to choose to die. But only that person should decide. If I was in a coma, I'd trust my family to decide to do what was best for me.

Richeal Drumgoole, 23
European Commission worker, Dublin
I find it very difficult to see how the law could be organised to cover every circumstance. Legalising euthanasia would mean that there was great scope for the abuse of power. For instance, it could be in the best interests of a family to get rid of a person in a coma.

Then you have to think of the doctors – many of them don't want to be put in the position of having to decide whether someone should live or die.

Rokhsana Fiaz, 26
Parliamentary officer, London
If I had an incurable disease I'd like the option of ending my life. Surely it should be possible to organise a system where you can state your wishes should your life ever be in the balance.

Therese Gram, 24
Psychology student, Denmark
I'm worried that old people would be put at risk if euthanasia was made legal and that it'd be open to abuse, especially if people didn't have the money to pay for private health care – relatives could be talked into pulling the plug just to save costs.

Dominic Williamson, 31
Charity worker, London
I'd hate to have the deciding vote on this one. If euthanasia was to be made legal, we'd have to have stringent guidelines to make sure that the power wasn't abused. I find the whole thing worrying – you might change your mind about dying just as they were sticking the lethal injection in!

Mike Hodson, 26
Van driver, Manchester
There are strong arguments against it. In some cases it's obvious that the person will never recover. But then again, there are patients who've seemed hopeless vegetables, then recover against all the odds. If you let them go, you're extinguishing all hope of recovery.

Ciorsdan Anderson, 23
Psychologist, London
If a person has left a 'living will' setting out their wishes in the event of a tragedy, then that should be respected. A friend of mine recently had a brain haemorrhage – he'd left instructions saying that he didn't want to be kept alive if there was no hope of recovery. I'm now considering making such a will myself.

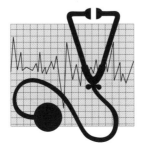

Zoe Lane, 24
Children's nanny, London
I believe that euthanasia should be legalised. Everyone should have the right to decide if they want to live or die. We should all sign something while we're still mentally alert.

Michelle Cattroll, 23
Hairdresser, Eastbourne
If euthanasia was legal it could be open to abuse. I think it's probably better to keep to the present system where doctors and families make quiet decisions to end someone's life if there's no hope. It's important that people are treated with dignity.

Thomas Stokke, 23
Mature student, London
I wouldn't want to be kept alive as a vegetable. But there'd have to be very strict rules if euthanasia was legalised. Ideally, you should have the consent of the person in that situation. That would mean they'd have to record their wishes while they're still in good health.

© EVA
June, 1998

The arguments for and against voluntary euthanasia

Against voluntary euthanasia

I warn you not to fall ill . . . not to grow old. By Cardinal Thomas Winning

A few elections ago, former Labour leader Neil Kinnock made one of the speeches of his life.

It didn't win him the popular vote, but it did go down as a great piece of rhetoric. It went something like this:

'If the Government win tomorrow, I warn you not to be disabled. I warn you not to fall ill and I warn you not to grow old.'

A decade on, I find myself repeating those warnings to alert people to the very real danger of sleepwalking into a future death sentence.

It's often said that for evil to triumph, all that is needed is for the good to do nothing. In the last few months too many people have done nothing – more through ignorance than apathy – and now a very real evil has triumph in its sights.

March 31 was the closing date for responses to a Government Green Paper entitled 'Who Decides?' on the finances and welfare of incapable adults.

The document contained many sensible suggestions for making sure the finances of people with dementia, those suffering from head injuries, patients in a coma and others were properly managed.

Its contents received little or no publicity.

Yet that widely-ignored paper contains some of the most frightening proposals ever drafted by legislators. Among the options it considers are:

Incorporating 'living wills' into the law of the land, which could prevent doctors carrying out life-saving treatment for fear of contravening the terms of such documents.

Provision for experiments to be carried out on patients, without their consent.

Allowing the withdrawal of feeding and fluids from patients, even those NOT deemed to be in a persistent vegetative state thus allowing them to die of thirst or starvation.

These provisions are not scare-mongering by an anti-euthanasia pressure group.

They are proposals offered for public discussion by our legislators, in this case the Lord Chancellor's Department.

I have agreed to lead a lobby of Parliament to implore our elected representatives to listen to our warnings. I want them to realise the consequences which could ensue, if they persist. I do not take this step lightly.

Many issues concern me; many groups ask for my support. But nothing I have seen in recent years poses a greater threat to our most basic notions of right and wrong.

Nazi experiments on their non-consenting victims are rightly deemed to be grotesque, yet we are now considering the legalisation of experiments on non-consenting, mentally incapable men and women.

We condemn death by starvation in the Nazi death camps, yet seem prepared to tolerate the death, by starvation, of patients in hospitals.

We wring our hands in anguish about animal experimentation, yet discuss plans to permit experiments on human beings.

What is being proposed is a subtle but nightmarish change in our basic notions of what is right and wrong.

Officially Britain is a country in which euthanasia is illegal, yet soon our hospitals could be brutalised and become death chambers.

The purpose of today's lobby of Parliament is to make more people aware of the dangers, to implore our legislators to step back from the abyss. If we are successful we will have done a service to humanity.

If not . . . 'I warn you not to be disabled. I warn you not to fall ill and I warn you not to grow old.'

• *Cardinal Thomas Winning is the leader of Scotland's Roman Catholics.*

For voluntary euthanasia

My right to choose the best way to die.
By Dr Jean Muir

From the distress I have seen in others through their degenerative conditions and suffering, I became a supporter of the campaign for voluntary euthanasia.

I have made a 'living will' saying that if I become incurably ill I do not want my life to be prolonged.

I made my decision after my father died from cancer following a long illness, and another terminally ill relative was kept alive against her wishes.

Watching the distress of close relatives disintegrating in the terminal stages of illness, and explicitly asking for a 'way out', convinced me euthanasia – or what I describe as a 'good' death – should be available to those who wish it.

One much-loved, elderly and extremely frail relative said that, for her, tomorrow would never come.

Without consultation, she was given antibiotics for her life-threatening pneumonia. She recovered, only to return to her original miserable state.

This event was, of course, not unique and similar situations may be becoming more common with all the technology available.

My living will is now signed and witnessed, with copies held by my sympathetic GP and my understanding family.

Most terminally ill people whose sufferings are relieved by the excellent care given by hospices, hospitals, GPs and other community services do not require to make decisions about voluntary euthanasia.

It is only needed for those whose protracted pain is unrelieved by any form of care or whose bodily disintegration is beyond endurance.

Around five per cent of the terminally ill cannot cope even with the superb medical care they receive.

For others, such as those with motor neurone disease or one of the other conditions which leaves a person's brain alert but eventually shuts down their bodily functions and communication skills, a prolonged life is intolerable.

If such people make repeated, rational pleas for assistance to die, what is there to fear in legislation to permit a gentle, medically-assisted, end to life?

Arguments against voluntary euthanasia are easily dispelled.

The oft-quoted cases of severely deformed babies or people with dementia being vulnerable to such treatment are not valid.

The patient must be able to express his or her own wishes. People who cannot make independent rational decisions are not affected.

I respect the religious arguments but, as a Roman Catholic, I am daunted by the inflexibility of thought in my own church, which attempts to deny voluntary euthanasia to believer and non-believer alike.

And I am totally dismayed, in the midst of the entire debate, by the wilful confusion of voluntary euthanasia with any other form of accelerated death.

It is the will of the person who is ill – and not imposed by any one else.

One grain of comfort lies in the respect now widely shown for living wills. They do not involve euthanasia, voluntary or otherwise.

A living will simply lets one's doctor know – in advance and in writing – that you do not wish your life to be artificially extended if you have an incurable, terminal illness or that you do not wish to delay an inevitable death by life-support procedures.

Such a directive is not yet legally binding, but there is a widespread hope that in the near future, Parliamentary legislation will make it so.

• Dr Jean Muir, 60, is a retired former general practitioner and Inverness hospital pathologist.

There is a powerful case for legalising assisted dying

Information from the Voluntary Euthanasia Society

The Voluntary Euthanasia Society was set up in 1935 by a group of doctors, lawyers and churchmen. Our aim is to make it legal for an adult, who is suffering unbearably from an incurable illness, to receive medical help to die at their own considered and persistent request. This means they must have persistently asked for medical help and were considered mentally able to do so. Safeguards include:

- getting a second medical practitioner to diagnose and predict the outcome of the illness;
- having a psychiatric assessment;
- having advice about the treatment and care which is available;
- being told all the necessary information before the choice is made; and
- writing a written request.

Our case for legalising assisted dying is set out below.

The right to decide

We believe that everyone has the right to choose how they live and die. Each person has value and is worthy of respect, has basic rights and freedoms and the power to control his or her destiny. As Professor Ian Kennedy wrote in 1988: 'Perhaps the most fundamental precept of the common law is respect for the liberty of the individual. In a medico-legal context this means that

a person's right to self-determination, to deal with his body as he sees fit, is protected by law. The doctor's first duty is to respect this right. This applies as much to the terminally ill patient as to any other.'

Passive euthanasia versus active euthanasia

At the moment, doctors can legally practise 'passive' euthanasia – that is, taking away or withholding treatment even if the person will die. However, doctors cannot directly help the person to die, for example, by giving a lethal injection. We argue that passive euthanasia has exactly the same moral and practical result as giving a lethal injection.

Quality of life – pain is not the only issue

Not everyone dies well. At least 5% of terminal pain cannot be fully controlled, even with the best care. Other distressing symptoms such as sickness, incontinence or breathlessness cannot always be relieved. But pain is certainly not the only issue in decisions about the end of life. What a patient thinks about their quality of life is often far more important. Many people do not want to spend the last days or weeks of their life in a way which, to them, is undignified.

Annie Lindsell, a campaigner for legalising assisted dying, said before she died of Motor Neurone Disease in 1997:

'The hospice movement consistently maintains that in most cases it manages the pain of terminally ill patients. What they cannot control, however, is the loss of personal dignity and that is a very individual criterion which no one but the patient can comment on.'

Having the power to take control over their own life and death can help people to keep a measure of human dignity in the face of their suffering. In 1995, sociologists Julia Addington-Hall and Clive Seale carried out an academic study into what patients with terminal cancer thought about dying. They said:

'Requests for euthanasia may indicate not that patients are giving up in the face of suffering, but that they are positively asserting their desire to control events.'

Euthanasia goes on already!

At the moment, the law and current medical practice do not match up. In 1994 a survey published in the *British Medical Journal* showed that some doctors already help patients to die. Few doctors have been prosecuted and, like Dr Cox, who was convicted of attempted murder in 1992, they have always been treated with great sympathy. Doctors are also legally able to give pain-relieving treatment in such high doses that people may die more quickly. This is known as the 'double effect' – relieving the patient's suffering is the accepted consequence of such treatment, with death as an unintended outcome.

Public opinion

Since 1950 when the first opinion poll was carried out, there has been a steady increase in public support for a change in the law. In the 1996 British Social Attitudes Survey, 82% of British people agreed with voluntary euthanasia.

Just one possible option at the end of life

Making it legal to help a person to die does not threaten the hospice movement. Assisted dying should be just one of the options at the end of life. In the Northern Territory of Australia, following the passing of a law to allow voluntary euthanasia, the budget for palliative care services was increased ten times over. This was to make sure that palliative care was available to everyone. Dr Pieter Admiraal, a well-known Dutch supporter of voluntary euthanasia, has repeatedly stressed that there should be: 'No euthanasia without palliative care.'

What are the arguments against assisted dying?

Only God can give and take away life

Some people believe that life is sacred and that no one has the right to purposely take a life. Many religious people follow this principle, so do not agree with suicide and assisted dying. However, there are many religious people who do support voluntary euthanasia, such as our vice-president Lord Soper, an important Methodist minister. In the Netherlands, Catholic or Dutch Reformed clergymen may be present at assisted deaths. It must also be remembered that religious arguments cannot, and should not, apply to anyone who does not share that belief.

The slippery slope – voluntary euthanasia will soon lead to involuntary euthanasia

This argument states that once we have made voluntary euthanasia legal, society will soon allow involuntary euthanasia. This is based on the idea that if we change the law to allow a person to help somebody to die, we will not be able to control it. This is misleading and inaccurate – voluntary euthanasia is based on the right to choose for yourself. It is totally different from murder. There is no evidence to suggest that strictly controlled voluntary euthanasia would inevitably lead to the killing of the sick or elderly against their will. As Ronald Dworkin, Professor of Law at Oxford and New York universities, said in 1994:

'Of course doctors know the moral difference between helping people who beg to die and killing those who want to live. If anything, ignoring the pain of terminally ill patients pleading for death rather than trying to help them seems more likely to chill a doctor's human instincts.'

People who do not agree with voluntary euthanasia often refer to the 1967 Abortion Act. They argue that the number of abortions which now take place every year shows that the safeguards set out in the Abortion Act have been ignored. They argue that this example should be taken as a warning of what could happen if helping people who are terminally ill to die is made legal. They believe that the law would not be able to control a huge amount of euthanasia cases, many of which would be involuntary.

However, abortion is a very different issue to assisted dying. It is also important to remember that people choose to have abortions, they are not forced on people. There is no evidence to suggest that assisted dying will be forced on anyone either.

It will have a damaging effect on society

Some people who do not agree with voluntary euthanasia argue that if it was legalised, it would damage the moral and social foundation of society by removing the traditional principle that man should not kill, and reduce the respect for human life. However, the idea that we should not kill is not absolute, even for those with religious beliefs – killing in war or self-defence is justified by most. We already let people die because they are allowed to refuse treatment which could save their life, and this has not damaged anyone's respect for the worth of human life.

Fear of abuse of the law

In any law which allowed a person to help someone to die, there would be safeguards to make sure that:

- the person is told everything about the process;
- they are not forced into making a decision; and
- they are mentally able to make the decision.

At the moment, no one knows how much non-voluntary euthanasia is carried out because active euthanasia is practised outside the law. In 1996 researchers from Monash University, Australia, carried out a study comparing end-of-life decisions in Australia, where voluntary euthanasia is illegal, and Holland, where it is permitted. They found that non-voluntary euthanasia actually took place five times more often in Australia.

Patients receive excellent palliative care, so euthanasia is unnecessary

Hospices do a wonderful job, making terminally ill patients comfortable and relieving their pain, but even experts in palliative care agree that not all pain can be fully controlled. Even if pain could be fully controlled, for many patients it is other parts of their condition, such as losing their dignity, that lead them to consider an assisted death. Palliative care cannot entirely replace the need for voluntary euthanasia. Some people will always want this choice.

Any change in the law must look at concerns about abuse of the law, but such fears should not prevent us from acting. As Ronald Dworkin, Professor of Law at Oxford and New York universities, said in 1994:

' . . . It would be perverse to force competent people to die in great pain or in a drugged stupor for that reason, accepting a great and known evil to avoid the risk of a speculative one.'

• The above is an extract from a series of factsheets on euthanasia issues, produced by the Voluntary Euthanasia Society. See page 41 for address details.

© *Voluntary Euthanasia Society, November, 1998*

...TRY AND THINK OF HER AS SHE WAS...

–BIT HARD WHEN THIS IS HOW SHE IS...

SIMON KNEEBONE

The case against euthanasia

Information from the Society for the Protection of Unborn Children (SPUC)

Medical homicide

The term *euthanasia* (derived from the Greek for 'good death') has come to mean the deliberate killing of sick or disabled persons for supposedly merciful reasons ('mercy killing').

The case against euthanasia

SPUC opposes euthanasia because:

- it is the deliberate killing of innocent human beings – a violation of the right to life
- it is contrary to medical ethics, putting doctors in the role of killers
- it assumes that the lives of the gravely ill and disabled are of less value than the lives of others

Patient autonomy and the right to life

The case for euthanasia is often argued on the basis of autonomy: the patient's freedom to make decisions about his or her own treatment. However, to invoke autonomy in this way involves a misunderstanding of the concept of autonomy, overlooking the principle that the patient's freedom entails a responsibility to act ethically. While a patient is capable of giving valid consent, a doctor has no authority to treat the patient unless that consent is given. But the patient cannot ethically refuse treatment with the intention to bring about his own death.

The ethical objection to suicide is reflected in law. In Britain, for compassionate reasons, there are no legal penalties for a person who attempts suicide, but assisting a suicide remains an offence. (Parliament recognised that people who have tried to kill themselves need help, not punishment.) Thus there is no legal right to suicide, and certainly no right to involve others in killing oneself. This is because the right to life is an inalienable right – no one may dispose of an innocent person's life, and so one cannot, in justice, intentionally deprive oneself of life.

Moreover, if the law were to allow some individuals to volunteer for euthanasia, this would also threaten the right to life of others, especially the elderly, the gravely ill and the disabled. Legalisation of euthanasia would make a clear statement to society that it was permissible for private citizens (e.g. doctors) to kill because they accepted the view that a patient's life was no longer worthwhile. If it is seen as a benefit to kill patients who consent to euthanasia, it is easy to argue that others should not be denied the same 'benefit' simply because they cannot ask for it. The fact that courts in Britain and other countries have already judged that some incapacitated patients may be starved to death challenges the notion that euthanasia would remain 'voluntary' if allowed by statute law.

Euthanasia versus good medical practice

Our opposition to euthanasia does not mean that we insist on 'medical treatment at all costs'. The alternative to euthanasia is good medical practice, which requires doctors to recognise when it is appropriate not to continue a particular treatment.

Sometimes a distinction is made between active euthanasia (e.g. a lethal injection) and passive euthanasia (withholding or withdrawing treatment). However, it is misleading to describe withholding or discontinuing treatment as 'euthanasia' unless this is done with the intention of killing the patient. Sometimes a treatment may properly be withdrawn even though the patient has consented to it, for example, when it is futile, merely prolonging the dying process in a terminally ill patient.

Likewise, the doctor's intention is the critical distinction between euthanasia and good palliative care (treatment to relieve distressing symptoms). For example, the dosage of painkillers necessary to control a patient's pain may have the side-effect of shortening his life. No moral objection arises as long as the drugs are not given with the intention of hastening the patient's death, but only in order to control the pain.

Tube-feeding and the 'persistent vegetative state'

In several countries (including Britain) courts have authorised the withdrawal of tube-feeding from patients with severe brain damage who are said to be in a 'persistent vegetative state' (PVS). This amounts to euthanasia if done with the intention of bringing about the patient's death. Tube-feeding does

AS DOCTORS OUR ROLE IS TO DO EVERYTHING WE CAN FOR YOU...

...FOR THE LONGEST POSSIBLE TIME...?

SIMON KNEEBONE

not become futile because it is thought that a patient has no awareness and will not recover (a judgement which is becoming increasingly questionable). Tube-feeding is not (in general) unduly burdensome, and only becomes futile if it no longer enables a patient to receive nourishment. Even if the provision of food and water require medical assistance, they are not intended to cure illness but are the basic means of sustaining life, which it is unjust to deny anyone on grounds of their disability.

Advance directives

Advance directives are statements by a patient which typically contain instructions that in the event of certain conditions arising (such as paralysis, incontinence, inability to communicate, the need for artificial life support) treatment should not be given. An advance directive is not necessarily a request for eu-thanasia, but such statements can be used to demand that doctors bring about the patient's death, for example, by specifying that tube-feeding should be withheld. For this reason advance directives (which in this context are often referred to as 'living wills') have become a focal point in the campaign of the pro-euthanasia lobby. The fact that legislation for living wills would facilitate the introduction of eu-thanasia is the principal reason why SPUC opposes moves in Parliament to make advance directives legally binding.

Furthermore, doctors might act on an advance directive in cir-cumstances which the patient did not foresee, or misinterpret the patient's wishes. While advance directives may be helpful to doctors in forming an impression of the patient's preferences, if binding they are liable to tie the hands of doctors, preventing them from acting in the patient's best interests. A patient may not realise that withholding treat-ment will not necessarily lead to an earlier death with less suffering: it may, in fact, lead to a bed-bound state with greater impairment of health.

When does life end?

Despite the convincing evidence that human development begins at fertilisation, moral debate on right-to-life issues has often been cast in terms of a controversy as to when life begins. Ironically, the question of when life ends is potentially far more contentious, as it is certainly more difficult (though by no mean impossible) to define.

The criterion of 'brain stem death' was originally intended to determine that death was imminent and inevitable, so that treatment should be discontinued. However, there has been a widespread tendency to regard this assessment as a diagnosis of death itself. Some commentators have gone further, suggesting that patients with certain forms of brain damage, such as persistent vegetative state, should be regarded as dead.

There is increasing concern among pro-life doctors and ethicists that a patient should not be regarded as dead until there is evidence of both brain stem death and the end of other vital functions. This would be a safeguard against ending the lives of patients who have volunteered for organ donation, before natural death has in fact occurred.

• For more information please contact SPUC whose address can be found on page 41.

The debate that refuses to die

Should we allow people the choice of when to die? The debate over euthanasia comes up periodic-ally but even when it isn't front page news, as when a doctor is being investigated or charged, it still rumbles on in the background.

Most recently there was the story of Dr Jack Kevorkian in America who was shown on a television documentary giving fatal injections to a patient who died on camera. Dr Kevorkian wants eu-thanasia legalised and challenged police to arrest him.

As an issue, euthanasia refuses to die. Everyone has an opinion on it; many would like to see a change in the law. Until it is properly debated it's not going to go away.

I can't recall there ever being a serious, informed debate on the

By Ray Mallon

subject in this country, and yet there is a strong lobby in the medical profession that would like to see change. It's time the Government, doctors, the law lords and the clergy examined the arguments and issues.

> *As an issue, euthanasia refuses to die. Everyone has an opinion on it; many would like to see a change in the law. Until it is properly debated it's not going to go away*

In my view there are three main sides to the debate: the people involved, the law and the moral/ religious side. Each one raises significant questions and arguments.

As a police officer and son of a funeral director, I have seen more death than most people. I have come into contact with many relatives who have lost loved ones, many who have died of cancer. Obviously the pain at losing a close relative is often deeply felt. The person is gone and we have to learn to live without them.

But often the greater trauma is having to watch people suffer and to look on helplessly with no chance of easing their pain.

Once they have passed away, the surviving family and friends' good memories may be clouded with the sadness of recalling how their loved one's final days were spent in agony and misery. And all they could do was watch them suffer and see them stripped of all dignity.

As far as the legal side is concerned, euthanasia is against the law. It is murder. Simple.

The law is dictated by the moral and religious argument. In the Ten Commandments, thou shalt not kill. But, as with other areas of life, society gives ground as the years pass and we become more tolerant and accepting of people's needs. Years ago who could have imagined a time when police officers would support the legalisation of taking cannabis and prostitution, as we see today?

With euthanasia, there is a growing number of doctors who want it to be legal in certain circumstances. I suspect there are many more who would like to speak out in favour of it but are too afraid to do so for fear of frightening their patients.

We may agree with them, we may disagree, but who can really know how they feel about euthanasia until they are faced with the situation of a relative who is terminally ill and in great pain who wants to die? I certainly can't come to a conclusion in this column as to how I would feel in that situation.

But I do know that if we have a dog or a cat that is suffering we call out the vet and have it put to sleep. Invariably the owner, although upset at the loss, feels better because the animal has been put out of its misery.

I'm not suggesting for one minute that we look at human life in the same way; we like to think we are treated better than animals. But which is better: letting people suffer but live longer, or allowing them to die in peace? It's an issue that's too hot for me to handle.

It needs a lot more thought and comment than I can come up with.

The time will come though when the Government will have to address euthanasia, and serious debate will have to begin. Otherwise, like a terminal disease it will continue to linger. *© The Northern Echo November, 1998*

Public support will change the law

Information from the Voluntary Euthanasia Society

Media polls regularly record huge majorities of people who support legalising voluntary euthanasia for the incurably ill. In October 1997, out of nearly 3,000 people who took part in a *Sun* newspaper telephone opinion poll, an amazing 97% said terminally ill people should have the right to die with dignity. The graph below shows the results of large scale statistical surveys on the topic carried out for us by NOP (National Opinion Polls).

We asked: 'Some people say that the law should allow adults to receive medical help to an immediate peaceful death if they suffer from an incurable physical illness that is intolerable to them, provided they have previously requested such help in writing. Please tell me whether you agree or disagree with this?'

It is clear that a large majority agreed, and this number is growing every year. The 1993 poll showed that sex, age, region or economic class made little difference to people's views on this subject. And the majority of people from all religious groups were in favour of voluntary euthanasia.

In 1996, Britain's largest social research institute carried out an independent survey into the social attitudes of British people. The survey showed that 82% of British people agreed with doctors helping patients to die if they have a disease which cannot be cured. They also support making such help legal.

It's no accident!

Those people who do not agree with their findings often criticise the wording of these polls. But not even people who are against assisted dying

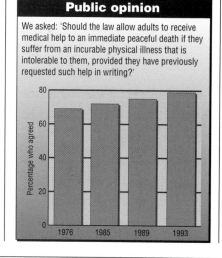

Public opinion

We asked: 'Should the law allow adults to receive medical help to an immediate peaceful death if they suffer from an incurable physical illness that is intolerable to them, provided they have previously requested such help in writing?'

can produce opinion poll results which are against voluntary euthanasia. In 1987, the British Section of the World Federation of Doctors Who Respect Human Life, who do not agree with voluntary euthanasia because of their religious beliefs, carried out a MORI poll. Overall, 72% of those surveyed said that voluntary euthanasia should be made legal.

Around the world

These figures are also shown in other countries. In the USA support for legalising voluntary euthanasia, as shown by Gallup poll results, has grown from 37% in 1947 to 75% in 1996. The Australian polls also back these results, with public support for voluntary euthanasia rising from 47% in 1962, to 78% in 1995. All round the world, voluntary euthanasia is supported by most people!

• The above is an extract from a series of factsheets on euthanasia issues, produced by the Voluntary Euthanasia Society. See page 41 for address details.

© Voluntary Euthanasia Society, 1998

Why my father had to die

Julia Sinclair's father was forceful, heroic and brilliant, but he died a crumpled man, bowed by cancer. She spent the last weeks at his bedside and the experience transformed her attitude to euthanasia

It was an April afternoon when my father fell ill. My mother came home to find him asleep. The air in his bedroom was hot and meaty. He had drawn the curtains tight against the spring sunshine. She knew something was wrong because only the day before he had been striding round his beloved garden, pruning shrubs and training clematis as usual. He was usually in the garden by six in the morning and stayed there till it was dark. Taking to his bed was an aberration which suggested we should worry but nothing could have prepared us for the weeks that followed.

By the time my father was diagnosed with cancer, a few days later, it had spread from his liver to his spine. There was nothing that could be done to stop it. All we could do was wait for his death. That wait was to turn my attitude towards euthanasia upside down.

Initially he was taken to a local hospital. The young ambulancemen who came to carry him away were reassuringly strong and jolly but my father would not let them touch him till he had 'tidied up'. His hands trembled as he tried to drag a comb through his fine raven hair, streaked with silver. I felt sorry for him and angry with these intruders, bulky in the little bedroom, with their professional smiles and polished bedside manners. They joked as they carried him down the narrow staircase. He looked as if he weighed no more than a dry leaf, tiny and crumpled in the stretcher, ashamed rather than frightened.

The local hospital failed to diagnose the cancer straight away. They dismissed the symptoms as typical of a dehydrated geriatric. The word 'geriatric' was a shock. My father was 73 and proud to have been in hospital only once, to remove a piece of shrapnel which had stuck in his gut, unnoticed since the war. He was

a bully, a superb raconteur, an intellectual show-off, a roaring drunk, an articulate opinionated writer, a voracious reader. And now we were confronted with a forlorn old man smelling of fear and rot.

The day he was diagnosed he told my mother not to tell us, his children. He never admitted he had cancer to my brother or me before he died. He only told my mother because she had recently been diagnosed with breast cancer herself and was undergoing treatment. He made a great show of being cheerful and pretended he felt marvellous.

He came home briefly before being moved to a London hospital for specialist treatment. Our local doctor came round for a drink and a chat. My mother, brother and I gathered in the drawing room to entertain him. We all felt rather hysterical and laughed a lot. It was a glorious, golden May day. The doctor told us that there was nothing he or anyone in his profession could do. He drank rather a lot of whisky. We smoked cigarettes ceaselessly and poured wine as if we were having a party. Like so many people who knew my father slightly, the doctor had

grown to admire him and now counted him as a friend. We ended up comforting him as much as he comforted us.

My father's stay at the London hospital was short-lived. I visited him there one muggy Sunday afternoon. The windows of his room were closed and the room stank. All the flowers were dead, the water slimy and putrid in the vases. In the bathroom a pair of soiled pyjama-bottoms lay on the floor. The bedclothes had not been changed. He was sweating. One of his ears was infected and oozed a sticky brown discharge into his pillow. A nurse told me briskly it was up to the relatives to worry about patients' clean pyjamas. Furthermore, she said, my father was a 'difficult' man. What he was mainly being difficult about was being bathed – he loathed his frailty and having to depend on nurses to wash him. He preferred to wait for my brother to come and give him his bath. He was miserable in that expensive, efficient, cold-hearted hospital. Our old family doctor, long since retired but still a friend, told us it was too late for medicine. He told us we should take him home.

So we did. Once home, my father was quite determined to dress and come downstairs daily, if only to sit in his favourite sofa and look out at the garden. He negotiated the stairs on his bottom, clutching whomever was at hand to break his fall while shouting at us to stop fussing. Each night he crawled upstairs to bed. When the skin on his knees and shins gave way and made this impossible, he sent us out for cricket pads.

Finally, the skin on his knees could not take the pressure, even through the padding. The flesh on the bone turned to a yellow septic pulp which seeped blood. So he retired upstairs to die. By now it was June and the weather was glorious. In the yellow bedroom we combed his hair each morning and tried to make food tempting enough for him to eat. He ate melon and sugary cereals and smoked, often burning the sheets and scorching the blankets when he fell asleep, stub in thin, fluttering fingers. He was skeletal and his skin so fragile that just touching him could break it and draw blood. Turning him was terrible because it hurt him so much. He had a morphine drip inserted permanently in his arm.

We were grateful for the nurses who came to live with us towards the end. The last was an Australian called Katie. We were acutely aware that she must have a life outside our house of illness and impending death, though we found it hard to imagine the ordinary pulse of daily life. We'd spent weeks in limbo, circling my father's bed. Because of Katie we sat down to eat regularly and forced ourselves to talk about the outside world. Such mundane routines kept us sane.

My father still refused to admit to us he was ill. Even now, we all went along with the idea that this was a minor illness. Contradicting him made him furious and his anger, even now, was potent.

My relationship with him had not always been easy and there were times when we had violently disagreed. His approach to fatherhood was old-fashioned. He felt his role was to provide for us and keep us safe and with me, his only daughter, he was passionately protective. Imagine then how he felt when I had to lead him, tottering and brittle-boned, to the loo and minister to him. I felt his whole body tremble with the shame.

During the last few days the pain became unspeakable. Till now he'd only admitted being afraid to Katie. But as the pain worsened, the fear began to show. He became agitated about knowing where we were. He told me he thought my latest television documentary, which had been broadcast while he was in hospital, 'wasn't at all bad'. He showed an interest in my brother's marketing business. He stopped shouting at my mother when she fussed lovingly round him.

Yet when it came to dying, choice and dignity were officially denied him even though his Living Will clearly stated what he wanted

---

Our house was a small old cottage and at night the slightest sounds were loud. My bedroom was across the corridor from my father's. During the last nights he started to scream with the pain. He swore too in a thick stream of filthy words. He was utterly humiliated by his loss of control. None of us slept but he wouldn't abide us in his room at night.

I was relieved because I couldn't bear to watch. This was my father, a man who'd flown Spitfires in the war and here he was boiled down to this shrunken, crumpled bundle of sores and bones. It was simply unbearable. In the wardrobe his immaculate suits hung pressed and in a chest of drawers, his silk shirts lay in their pristine wrappings, his Garrick ties folded, his handkerchiefs ironed. It was the pathetic sight of his shoes that finally cracked me. Those old-fashioned, lace-up, hand-made shoes, buffed till they gleamed, were redolent of status and importance. They were the shoes of a swaggering, thriving man with people to see and places to go. And they were lined up like soldiers just inches from where my diminished father lay dying.

Then my father cracked too. He just wanted the pain to end. He begged us to make it stop. The third night none of us even pretended to sleep. Our regular doctor was on holiday in Spain. We called another. He arrived at 2am, tired and hot on this beautiful summer night in a rumpled pair of shorts. He looked no more than about 20. He was confronted by two women, begging for an end to the pain. My mother, in a shabby pink dressing gown that made me weep, produced my father's Living Will and begged the doctor to act upon it. The doctor said he couldn't up the dose of morphine without it being 'dangerous'. What were the alternatives? For my father to hold out for another day perhaps and die, unable to focus on anything outside the constricted corner of his pain?

The young doctor could see there was nothing he could do for my father except to give him a lethal dose of morphine – any less would not have stopped the pain. He knew he was doing something illegal and therefore 'wrong' but in the face of such pain, his moral certainties withered. He administered the necessary dose.

My father died the next morning. He regained consciousness and smiled – it seemed weeks since he'd done so. My mother and I held a hand each and he looked into our eyes for the last time.

He died at home, surrounded by his family. He'd lived to be 73. Really, compared with millions, he was very lucky. Yet when it came to dying, choice and dignity were officially denied him even though his Living Will clearly stated what he wanted. My mother, who has recovered from cancer, is not terrified of being denied a dignified, pain-free death. I have a copy of her Living Will plus detailed instructions of how to find the spare copy in case she falls ill. If she becomes terminally ill and experiences pain, why shouldn't she have the death she's asked for in advance and in writing? Who is anyone to play God and deny her?

© *Independent on Sunday*
December, 1998

Cast-iron argument for not giving up

Just over a decade ago Kathy Sargent would have accepted euthanasia to end her illness-ravaged life but, as Alan Cocksedge has discovered, experimental treatment put her on the road to recovery and blossoming artistic interests

As a youngster, Kathy Sargent always wanted to own a pony – but being one of five children her family could not run to such an expense.

Now she has used her own developing talents as an artist and sculptor to create her very own four-legged friend.

The Welsh pony has just been put out to graze on the front lawn of her family home in Pot Kiln Road, Great Cornard, and council officials say the eye-catching animal will need no planning approval – unless its creator decides to start charging people to view her work.

Spurred on by her initial success, Kathy, who fought back from the brink of death following illness a few years ago, says she will not be stopping at one horse on her lawn, and is already getting ready to produce a larger model.

The 45-year-old mother also wants her work to act as a sculptural beacon to others who may be suffering illnesses from which they are tempted to feel they will never recover. Within a few days of putting her first cast-iron pony, named Grand Creator – an anagram of Great Cornard – in her garden, she has already received many words of praise for her creativity from neighbours and passers-by.

'I love animals and would be quite happy to fill my front garden with them,' confesses Kathy, who works weekends as a relief warden at Babergh District Council's Playford Court sheltered home unit in Sudbury.

Having enjoyed art at Sudbury High School, but never having done any more after leaving full-time education, she decided five years ago to take a part-time, two-year course at Colchester Institute to gain a visual studies Certificate in Higher Education. At that time she was working on a supermarket check-out, but also decided to take on the role of a student while her two teenaged children were studying for university. Later, husband Cliff, an engineering factory employee, also joined the family learning curve experience by studying how to weld in order to create the main frames for Kathy's sculptural efforts. Her studies at Colchester enabled her to become a proficient painter of animals, and she takes on numerous commissions for pet owners, signing her works under her maiden name of Hart. She

became hooked on sculpturing three years ago after attending a week-long course at the Chattisham studio of Ipswich sculptor and lecturer Miles Robinson. She went on to make mantlepiece-size animals, and has since been attending the same studio weekly in a two-year exercise to rear Grand Creator – her first life-sized piece.

Her development as a sculptress follows developing intestinal Crohn's disease when she was 30.

'The potentially fatal disease, which causes inflammation, thickening and ulceration of various parts of the bowel, initially affected me when I weighed 11 stone. Within three years I was down to seven stone, and I was in such a terrible condition by then that my husband would have allowed me to accept voluntary euthanasia, had it been legal.

'I had been treated with steroids, but was dying, and in such pain I could not even bear to be laid in bed. My bones were sticking out through my skin and I could not eat. We then decided to go privately to see retired gastroenterologist Dick Arden-Jones, who had previously worked in West Suffolk, but was then in Cambridge. He decided to reduce the number of

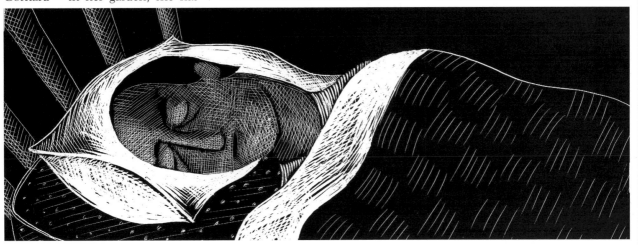

steroids I was taking and substitute them with Azathioprine, which is given to transplant patients to stop rejection. Within a short time the combination of drugs worked and I began regaining weight.

'Mr Arden-Jones charged me only for the initial consultation, but continued to look after me on a friendly, voluntary basis for many more years until his death two years ago at the age of 84. He regarded me as something of an experiment.

'He was interested in studying my case, and the belief that Crohn's disease involves the body rejecting the bowel. I continue to take the same combination of drugs.

'Because of what happened to me I am anxious to show to others suffering from any similar illnesses that they should not give up on life.

> *'Because of what happened to me I am anxious to show to others suffering from any similar illnesses that they should not give up on life'*

There always has to be hope round the corner. I believe what has happened to me proves it, but fully understand the reasons at the time of my family's thoughts of euthanasia.'

Husband Cliff, a technical operations manager with Lucas Varity, says he is proud of Kathy's achievements both in the way she has recovered from her illness and in her blossoming as a sculptress.

However, he says the family has no regrets in having flirted with ideas of euthanasia when at the depths of their despair 12 years ago.

'I had been thinking positively towards the principle of euthanasia some time before Kathy's illness, and when she appeared to be in such a hopeless and distressed position we would have seriously considered the option, had it been available. The fact she subsequently recovered does not alter my views on the subject.

'What is happening in our lives now is a bonus for which we are very grateful. Kathy has amazed me in what she has been doing, not just her sculpturing, but the way she has transformed our home with creative stencilling and other decorating.'

© East Anglian Daily Times
June, 1998

Lords warned over following Dutch road to euthanasia

By Philip Johnston, Home Affairs Editor

Concern that Britain could follow Holland along the road to widespread use of euthanasia was voiced in the House of Lords last night by one of the country's leading surgeons.

Lord McColl, the Professor of Surgery at Guy's Hospital of Surgery at Guy's Hospital, London, said there was evidence from the Netherlands to show that 'the current practice of euthanasia is out of control'.

Advocates of the 'right to die' often point to Holland as a model for how doctor-assisted voluntary euthanasia for terminally-ill patients can work without abuse.

But Lord McColl said the system of regulation was not working and pointed out the dangers of Britain adopting similar practices under a review of the law now taking place in Whitehall.

Last month, Church leaders expressed concern that plans to make 'living wills' legally enforceable marked a further step towards the acceptance of voluntary euthanasia. It is feared that the courts could be used to make case law that would bypass Parliament and allow doctors to assist the deaths of mentally-incompetent patients.

Lord McColl said that as a result of lenient judgments by Dutch courts, accepted medical practice changed and euthanasia became acceptable. 'By the time Parliament considered the matter in 1993, it was a case of attempting to shut the stable door after the horse had bolted,' he said.

He claimed that attempts were being made in Britain to mirror the position in Holland and cited last year's High Court action brought by Annie Lindsell, who suffered from motor neurone disease.

The action was supported by the Voluntary Euthanasia Society ostensibly to establish the sort of treatment her family doctor was entitled to give. In the event, the case collapsed because the court ruled the palliative care proposed was already legal.

But Lord McColl said: 'The purpose behind the Annie Lindsell case was to try to obtain permission to give an unlimited and unspecified dose of diamorphine which could have resulted in her immediate death and would then have been hailed as the first legal case of euthanasia in this country.

'How can we be sure that what happens in Holland today will not happen in this country tomorrow?'

Although euthanasia and assisted suicide strictly remain illegal in Holland, doctors who help patients to die will not be prosecuted provided they follow certain guidelines.

Lord Irvine, the Lord Chancellor, is considering whether to introduce laws to give statutory force to living wills, whereby an individual states what sort of treatment they would want should they fall seriously ill.

He said last month: 'The Government's opposition to euthanasia is settled, well-known and unqualified.'

© Telegraph Group Limited,
London 1998

Freed, the woman who helped her sick mother to die

Daughter calls for euthanasia rethink after 'exceptional' case. By Chris Brooke

A devoted daughter who helped her sick mother to die walked free from court yesterday and called for a rethink on euthanasia.

Gillian Jennison watched frail 83-year-old Annie Wilkes take 23 sleeping pills and later smothered her with a pillow.

The 53-year-old lecturer told police that her mother, who suffered from chronic dementia, had decided to die rather than go into a nursing home.

Sentenced to 12 months' probation, Jennison left Leeds Crown Court and said: 'The case of euthanasia now needs to be reviewed. My mother had asked me to end her suffering and I felt I had no other option but to help her.'

The divorced mother of two was originally charged with murder. But prosecution lawyers decided to accept a guilty plea to the lesser charge of aiding and abetting suicide.

James Goss, QC, told the court: 'The Crown is not in any way condoning actions such as this by relatives or those who care for the elderly. It is the appropriate course in the somewhat exceptional circumstances of this case.'

Jennison said last night: 'Although I broke the law I feel that I could do nothing else.'

Describing her mother as a 'very brave and self-reliant person', Jennison said: 'On the day she died she had finally learnt she would not recover. She said, "I don't want to go to a nursing home. I just want to die. Please give me the pills". And I said, "You will have to take them yourself".'

Mother and daughter talked until Mrs Wilkes went to sleep. Jennison then went and got rid of the empty packet of pills in a nearby skip 'which was an incredibly stupid thing to do'.

When she came back, her mother was still breathing. 'I got the

pillow and held it very gently and if my mother had struggled or stirred I wouldn't have continued but she didn't,' Jennison said.

'People who help others to die for the best, compassionate and good reasons are not murderers. My case was one small part of something that's an issue.'

'The case of euthanasia now needs to be reviewed. My mother had asked me to end her suffering and I felt I had no other option but to help her'

Earlier, judge Mrs Justice Smith said that Jennison had been 'overwhelmed' by her mother's death and that it was 'difficult to imagine the anguish' caused by the request to help her die. However, the daughter had had 'the courage to do what she did and the courage to speak of it'.

Jennison had not been motivated by wanting to avoid the burden of caring for an elderly relative, the judge said.

She warned: 'It must not be thought that where a friend or member of the family takes this kind of step it will necessarily be treated in the way I am intending to treat you.'

Mrs Wilkes had brought up two children after being widowed at 48. She worked hard to earn a living until retiring at 66.

An independent and determined woman, she found the onset of chronic dementia and the early stages of Alzheimer's Disease difficult to bear. It was in December 1996 that relatives noticed a dramatic deterioration in her health.

Mrs Wilkes lived alone in Cottingley, West Yorkshire, next to her sister-in-law. In April 1997 she was admitted to Westfield nursing home in Bingley where her daughter Gillian visited two or three times a day.

In June it was decided that Mrs Wilkes was capable of returning home with daily care help.

Mr Goss told the court that the elderly woman was 'quiet and withdrawn and a little bit depressed and fed up with life'. Her doctor prescribed sleeping tablets to help her cope. On July 18 Mrs Wilkes rang her sister-in-law next door saying 'she felt dreadful and very dizzy'.

Jennison, a lecturer in trade union law at Bradford College, came round immediately and took her mother back to her house in East Morton, near Keighley.

There, Mrs Wilkes's condition got even worse. 'She was seeing double, totally confused and could scarcely walk,' Jennison later told detectives.

That evening Mrs Wilkes's son Colin visited with his wife. He noticed that his mother looked 'frail, unwell and tired'.

Together the family drank wine and ordered a takeaway pizza. When Mrs Wilkes retired to bed upstairs her son took her sleeping tablets downstairs.

Later that night, when mother and daughter were left alone in the

_____

'People who help others to die for the best, compassionate and good reasons are not murderers. My case was one small part of something that's an issue'

_____

house, they began drinking sherry. It was then that Mrs Wilkes said she wanted to die and asked Jennison to get the sleeping pills, which she swallowed two or three at a time washed down with water.

When Jennison found later that her mother was still alive, she held the pillow against her face 'for a couple of minutes, not wanting to let her down', Mr Goss said.

Jennison told detectives: 'It all seemed to go quiet and her breathing stopped. She was dead.'

A post-mortem failed to establish whether the pills alone, the smothering with the pillow or a combination of both had killed Mrs Wilkes, the court heard.

After the hearing Josephine Quintavalle, of the anti-euthanasia group Life, said: 'It is a very worrying trend when we feel the only solution to difficulties that people may be having is to kill them.'

And Dr Peggy Norris, chairman of Alert, said: 'What's wrong with these judges? It is giving carte blanche to anyone to do the same. It's shocking and terrible discrimination against elderly people.'

The will to live

Mark cannot eat, move or talk: but the hardest part of his illness is convincing doctors that he wants to go on living

Ten-year-old Nadia leans forward, concentrating intently, her gaze never leaving her father's face. Slowly, one by one, Mark Foster mouths the individual letters of each word he wants to say: each movement has a nuance, each blink a meaning that his family has, through time, learnt to interpret.

In their laborious code, one blink means yes, two indicates no. It is painstaking and it is difficult. Each laborious movement is punctuated only by the nimble administrations of a nurse who must constantly clear the fluid which collects in Mark's lungs.

A single, short sentence can take many minutes. Nadia, waiting patiently for each instruction, is meticulous in her translation. This, she knows, is infinitely important to her father: it is his lifeline, his only means of communication.

Mark Foster has motor neurone disease (MND), a fatal degenerative condition that attacks the nervous system: sufferers rarely survive more than five years after diagnosis. His

quality of life is poor: he cannot eat, he cannot move, he cannot talk. His lungs need regular suctioning to help him breathe. He is not in pain, but he lives each day in terrifying circumstances. Alert and aware, he is trapped in a body that barely functions.

But Mark Foster desperately wants to live. He knows his time is limited and he knows he wants each moment of it. Yet his biggest battle to survive has been with the medical profession who have, in his opinion, urged him to let his precious life slip away, to die with what they consider 'dignity'.

_____

'Even if I only do the littlest thing with the children and teach them something each day, it was worth me being here'

_____

They have never suggested withholding treatment but, many times, they have implied that, perhaps, it may be the best way for him and for his family.

At times he has faltered. His slow descent into the frightening realms of terminal illness has terrified him: at times, it has sapped his will to survive. Yet he is determined that no one will take from him the life he has left. 'I have been to death and come out of the other side,' he says.

'Everything has a different colour now. Even if I only do the littlest thing with the children and teach them something each day, it was worth me being here.'

His story is one of inspiration, but also one that frighteningly illustrates the subtle pressure that exists for the terminally-ill to embrace euthanasia.

Even in his darkest moments, it has not been his appalling illness that has made him contemplate letting his life go – it has been the medical professionals. 'I think it is very interesting how I came round to the way I think now,' laboriously explaining through his wife, Nathalie.

'There was a time when I was going to give in. Not to the illness, but to the doctors. I felt they were encouraging me to go down the path of euthanasia. Now I think: "How dare they!"'

Propped up in an armchair in the sunny, yellow-walled living room of his north London flat, Mark gazes out of the window into the roomy aviary that dominates the garden. For hours he will watch the robins that flit behind the glass amid the dense vegetation. A garden designer, he loves to watch the passing seasons.

This is no invalid's ward. There is little paraphernalia of the sick room: instead, an overflowing basket of unironed laundry nestles amid the bath toys of his three children. Their paintings jostle for position on the noticeboards alongside family snaps, postcards and photographs of gardens Mark designed before he became ill in 1994. This is a happy family home.

As Nathalie sits by his chair, she occasionally moves his legs so that he is more comfortable. As she voices his words she constantly strokes his arm tenderly. 'People think that, even if they were half as ill as he is, they would want to die,' she says. Later, as she snatches a quick cigarette in the sanctuary of the kitchen, Nathalie talks of her joy in Mark's life. How his diminished health has not diluted their life together: 'I have thought about the meaning of life and to me it is about the chance to be together as a family and savouring the small things: drinking hot chocolate, thinking about when I'll next be sitting in the bluebells with Mark.

'You can't break someone down into bits – a brain, a beautiful pair of eyes: it is much deeper than that.'

When Mark was diagnosed, four years ago at 31, Nathalie was pregnant with their third child: it should have been an idyllic period in their marriage. Together they faced the full implications of his disease, determining to remain as optimistic about his outlook as possible. The medical profession, however, made that increasingly difficult.

'There was a time when I was going to give in. Not to the illness, but to the doctors. I felt they were encouraging me to go down the path of euthanasia. Now I think: "How dare they!"'

In the summer of 1997, Mark had to go into hospital for five weeks after a severe chest infection that ultimately cost him his voice. It was then that doctors first began talking of 'death with dignity'. Slowly, their urgings took a toll on his spirit and will.

'They did not break my spirit, but it was going down and they did not stop it,' Mark says. Looking back, Nathalie recalls her husband's demeanour as that of a man slowly being bludgeoned into submission: into acceptance of his death.

'His face reminded me of that pilot captured by the Iraqis during the Gulf war and paraded on television. He was not himself; his spirit was being broken.' There was, they felt, a strong sense of institutionalised pressure to surrender to death. To resist it required enormous energy.

'The doctor was very frank,' Mark recalls. 'He told me that I would die from the chest infection and maybe that would be better and a more dignified way to go.

'The other option was a tracheotomy and never talking again. I thought that was the worst thing to hear. But then he said I would also have to have a ventilator and was unlikely to come off it. I was given an hour to make a decision.'

Mark's choice was to go ahead with the surgery. As he was being wheeled into theatre, the couple quickly devised a means of at least crude communication. One blink for yes, two for no. Even then there were anxious moments. While the family prepared for their agonising wait there was a power cut at the hospital.

'It was significant for me that when my power was failing and it was getting dark, their power failed. It could not have been worse for my spirit,' Mark remembers.

Nathalie addressed her husband's flagging morale with vigorous determination, fearing it would adversely affect how the doctors assessed him. To convey his fighting spirit, she insisted everyone should read a slip of paper before they began. It was, in part, his final words to her before the operation. It said: 'Tell them I walked in here and I am going to walk out.'

The prevailing attitude on the ward – that Mark's death was the most likely and almost the most preferred outcome – worried her deeply. 'It wasn't until his spirit had healed that I wanted anyone to talk to him,' Nathalie says. 'I remember saying: "You should wait for my husband to recover from pneumonia before you start asking him if he wants to die [by offering him doses of diamorphine]."

'I wanted him to be able to take decisions in his right mind. If you don't eat for five days, you are heady. And if you feel sick and people start suggesting things, you are not in the best position to respond. I just wanted him to see things clearly.

'I also did not want them to judge him just on what he was at that time – flat on his back, unable to move and speak for himself. I was terrified they would write him off.'

There were other dispiriting indications, too, that doctors felt Mark's survival was a bad outcome, rather than a good one. One young doctor, Nathalie recalls, said patronisingly: 'Some relatives just can't bear to let their loved ones go.' Another doctor told her that he was surprised Mark had had the tracheotomy because it would keep him alive longer. Had he been the doctor, he said, he would not have done it.

Together with Mark's best friend, Matt, Nathalie began rebuilding her husband's confidence and spirits when he left hospital. A newspaper story recounting Jeremy Beadle's role in the assisted suicide of a friend with MND angered Mark and helped him regain his determination. 'I couldn't believe it when I read that the man could walk,' Mark says.

'I thought, what the hell is going on? He had a life to live for.' In contrast, when Mark was at his lowest, Matt encouraged him. 'He will always know he saved my life and that is a great thing to know,' Mark says.

Mark first confided his anger about Beadle's role in the assisted suicide to psychotherapist Josephine Speyer, the London co-ordinator of the Befriending Network.

Designed to provide non-medical support for the terminally-ill, the charity carefully matches each befriender and patient to ensure a close bond. For Mark, Josephine's friendship has helped strengthen his will to survive. 'The fact that someone says to me "see you next week" is everything to me,' he says. 'I have to learn to believe them.'

'I feel I have a happier life now, because I have learned to appreciate it to the full,' he says. 'And the children love having their father here'

From arranging regular sessions with Josephine to putting up a photograph of a Japanese garden that Mark had created, Nathalie and Matt helped Mark to plot the co-ordinates from despair to well-being. 'Little things started to heal him,' Nathalie says.

'Looking at the view of the trees together, that sort of thing.' Once, when Nathalie had taken her husband to the lavatory, he pretended to be dead. 'It was funny and horrible and frightening – but it meant he had got his sense of humour back,' she recalls. 'And that meant I had got him back.'

It was a turning point, Mark agrees. 'It meant I could laugh at the thought of dying. I remember looking at the trees and drinking in life from the outside.'

Today Mark's physical outlook is hardly less bleak. His will, however, to live the remainder of his life at his own pace, is intact. 'I feel I have a happier life now, because I have learned to appreciate it to the full,' he says. 'And the children love having their father here.'

There is no intricate, deep meaning to Mark's sense of survival, to his will to hold tight to the life that he has. His philosophy is simple. It is, he says: 'Pure love and you don't let anyone else endanger that.'

Attitudes to euthanasia

% who think euthanasia should 'definitely' or 'probably' be allowed by law for a person . . .

. . . who has an incurable illness which leaves them unable to make a decision about their **own** future, for instance imagine a person in a coma or on a **life-support machine** who is never expected to regain consciousness (if their relatives agree).	**86%**
. . . who has an incurable and painful illness from which they will die, for example, someone dying of cancer.	**80%**
. . . in a coma, never expected to regain consciousness, but who is **not** on a life-support machine (if their relatives agree).	**58%**
. . . who is not in much pain, **nor** in danger of death, but becomes permanently and completely **dependent** on relatives for all their needs, for example, someone who cannot feed, wash, or go to the toilet by themselves.	**51%**
. . . with an incurable illness from which they will die, but is **not** very painful, as might be the case for someone dying from leukaemia.	**44%**
. . . with an incurable illness from which they will **not** die, for example, someone with severe arthritis.	**42%**
. . . someone who is not ill or close to death, but who is **simply tired of living** and wishes to die – for example, someone who is extremely lonely and no longer enjoys life.	**12%**

Base: 1234

Source: 'Matters of life and death: attitudes to euthanasia' in British Social Attitudes the 13th Report SCPR 1996/97

What GPs really think about hastening death

As the debate on euthanasia intensifies, Louise McKee looks at evidence for a sea-change in GP attitudes.

The *Sunday Times* survey that claimed one in seven GPs has broken the law by helping patients to die at their request is but the latest event in a growing euthanasia debate.

The recent wave of doctors confessing to giving lethal doses of drugs to hasten the deaths of terminally ill patients began last year. Dr Michael Irwin, former medical director of the United Nations and a retired GP, admitted he had administered fatal doses to around 50 patients over a 40-year career.

Dr David Moor, a GP from Newcastle, was charged last year with the murder of an elderly patient.

Evidence suggests that attitudes towards euthanasia and physician-assisted suicide among the medical profession may be shifting, with more doctors willing to consider practising it regardless of the current legal situation.

The practice of euthanasia may be more commonplace than previously imagined. GPs readily admit that the topic is frequently raised by patients and relatives.

Half of the 200 GPs who responded to a confidential survey published in *Pulse* last November admitted to having eased a patient's death. Almost half the GPs said that they had been in a position where they felt that easing a patient's death was the right thing to do.

Many GPs saw hastening of death through 'double effect' as part of their duty – sometimes at a patient's request, but more frequently through the doctor's own compassion.

A survey of 221 GPs and 203 hospital doctors published in the *BMJ* (May 1994) found 91 per cent of doctors were willing to practise passive euthanasia – withdrawing treatment that prolongs life. They regarded it as a legitimate response to a patient's request.

Taking active steps to end a patient's life is, however, both illegal and against the recommendations of the BMA.

Many GPs and hospital doctors would like to see a change in this law.

Despite recent evidence of a 50-50 split in opinion between those for and against the legalisation of voluntary euthanasia, the number of GPs who have come out in support of a change in the law has grown over the last decade.

For instance, a National Opinion Poll survey of 301 GPs for the Voluntary Euthanasia Society in 1987 showed 30 per cent of GPs agreed with the concept of voluntary euthanasia. The findings showed, however, that a sizeable proportion of GPs would consider practising euthanasia, even though they themselves were not in favour of it.

A postal survey of 1,000 medical practitioners' attitudes towards physician-assisted suicide was carried out by Professor Sheila McLean of the Medical Law Unit, University of Glasgow, in 1996 – 12 per cent of the respondents were GPs.

In total, 55 per cent of respondents believed they should be allowed by law to assist the suicide of a patient who was either terminally ill or in a state of extreme mental or physical suffering.

Pharmacists and anaesthetists were the two professional groups who felt most strongly in favour of this (72 and 56 per cent respectively). GPs and other professional groups were more circumspect, with 48 per cent of GPs, surgeons, hospital physicians and psychiatrists favouring a change in the law.

A survey of 750 GPs and hospital doctors published in the *BMA News Review* (September 1996) confirmed there were deep splits of opinion in the medical profession.

While 46 per cent of doctors supported a change in the law to

allow them to carry out the request of a terminally ill patient for euthanasia, 44 per cent were against euthanasia and supported the present law.

Twenty-two doctors confessed to actually breaking the law by actively intervening to end the life of a terminally ill patient.

There is conflicting evidence as to how widespread the practice of physician-assisted suicide is among the medical profession.

Professor McLean's survey showed that while 28 per cent of respondents had been asked to provide the means for a patient to kill themselves, only 4 per cent actually complied by supplying drugs or information about various lethal acts.

Yet a higher proportion of doctors may be willing to break the law than those figures would suggest.

The *BMJ* survey showed 46 per cent of respondents would consider taking active steps to bring about the death of a patient if it were legal to do so.

Almost half of the doctors surveyed had been asked by a patient to take active steps to hasten death. A third of the doctors who had been

---

The argument 'it is wrong to take one's own life or to help someone else take theirs' was not judged to be particularly important

---

asked to take active steps had complied with a patient's request. Interestingly, GPs (30 per cent) were less likely than consultants (36 per cent) to comply with the patient's wishes, despite a higher proportion of GPs (64 per cent) than consultants (52 per cent) receiving such requests. The survey highlighted a dilemma experienced by some GPs.

While no association was found between a doctor practising active euthanasia and holding a religious belief, there was a strong association between a doctor holding a religious belief and believing that the law on euthanasia should not be changed. These doctors also stated that they would be unwilling to practise active euthanasia if it became legal.

The study authors concluded: 'The attitudes held by some doctors with religious beliefs seem to be at variance with their behaviour, implying painful, personal dilemmas.'

The strongest arguments from respondents against the introduction of physician-assisted suicide in Professor McLean's study were 'problems judging when suffering is sufficient to justify physician-assisted suicide' (53 per cent) and that 'many people who feel suicidal later regret those feelings' (50 per cent).

Other reasons cited were that 'patients sometimes recover from seemingly terminal conditions' and 'the families of patients might object or sue'.

The argument 'it is wrong to take one's own life or to help someone else take theirs' was not judged to be particularly important.

Arguments viewed as very important in favour of introducing physician-assisted suicide were that 'it is the duty of doctors to relieve suffering' (60 per cent) and 'some people suffer intolerable and incurable conditions' (59 per cent).

'In these responses we can detect conflicts between the felt duty of doctors to preserve life and to relieve suffering,' said Professor McLean.

© Pulse
November, 1998

Medical opinion

Doctors are essential in this debate

There is increasing medical interest and support in the United Kingdom for legalising voluntary euthanasia. In 1990, a working party from the Institute of Medical Ethics said: 'A doctor, acting in good conscience, is ethically justified in assisting death if the need to relieve intense and unceasing pain or distress caused by an incurable illness greatly outweighs the benefit to the patient of further prolonging his life.'

Official opinion supports the present law

At the moment, the British Medical Association (BMA) is against legalising voluntary euthanasia. At their 1997 conference they voted

against any immediate change in the law on assisted dying. However, they do support living wills and a patient's right to refuse treatment. In 1995 the BMA said: 'Recent legal cases have now shown beyond doubt that when an informed and competent patient makes an advance decision to refuse specific treatments which would otherwise be given later, that refusal will be legally binding on doctors.'

In July 1995, *The Lancet*, one of the main medical journals in the world, dealt positively with voluntary euthanasia. The article was called 'The Final Autonomy', and the final sentence read: 'All we ask is that Medicine moves towards non-medical opinion by admitting euthanasia openly (and more honestly) into all its future discussions of end-of life decisions affecting competent adults.'

Many doctors support a change in the law!

In the September 1996 issue of the BMA *News Review*, the results of a survey of over 750 GPs and hospital doctors showed that doctors were divided over legalising voluntary euthanasia. The results were as follows.

- 46% of doctors supported a change in the law to allow them to carry out the request of a terminally ill patient for euthanasia.
- 44% were against euthanasia and supported the present law.
- 37% said they would be willing to actively help to end the life of terminally ill patients who had asked for euthanasia, if the law allowed it.

Twenty-two doctors actually confessed to having broken the law and helped someone to die. Following this survey, Dr Stuart Horner, who was then the chairman of the BMA's medical ethics committee, said: '. . . if we genuinely believe that all the efforts of medicine have been exhausted it may well be that in a particular case euthanasia has to be considered. That is a matter for the doctor concerned and I would be the last person to say they had done the wrong thing.'

Nurses would also like to see a change in the law. In 1995, a survey carried out by the *Nursing Times* found that 68% of nurses believed that if people ask for help to end their life, it should be given in some circumstances. 69% of nurses had personal experience of a patient asking for voluntary euthanasia.

Doctors do carry out voluntary euthanasia!

In 1994, a report published in the *British Medical Journal* showed that British doctors do practise voluntary euthanasia, despite the law. The study by B. J. Ward and P. A. Tate, from Cambridge University, found that 32% of doctors surveyed had agreed to a patient's request to be given treatment to help them die more quickly. A larger proportion – 46% – said they would consider giving treatment to help someone die if it were legal to do so.

In November 1997, 200 GPs responded to a survey carried out by

Today, the growing support of the medical profession for assisted dying will eventually help to change the law

Pulse magazine. The survey revealed that 93 GPs (47%) had given treatment to ease a patient's death. 49% said that they had been in a position where they felt that easing a patient's death, other than with the intention of relieving symptoms only, was the right thing to do.

What about the Hippocratic Oath?

The Hippocratic Oath was established around 2,500 years ago in Greece. Some doctors use it as a guide to carrying out their work. Part of the Hippocratic Oath states: 'I will neither give a deadly drug to anybody if asked for it, nor will I make a suggestion to this effect.' A doctor who follows this Oath also promises 'not to give a woman a pessary to produce abortion'. However, abortion is now legal in some circumstances, and many doctors perform this operation. The Oath has been changed and updated to fit in with new attitudes and medical practices – it is not a code which cannot be altered. At the moment, the BMA is campaigning to update the oath. They argue that it does not reflect the reality of medical practice today. They want the code to recognise that keeping people alive is not the only aim of health care. As R. Weir wrote in 1992: 'The achievement of . . . appropriate medical goals is more important than a literal adherence to an ancient oath whose religious and moral framework is of such limited relevance to contemporary medicine that the oath is frequently altered when used in medical school convocations and increasingly replaced entirely by other kinds of oaths, including those written by medical students themselves.'

It is important to remember that the Voluntary Euthanasia Society was set up by a group of doctors and clergy in 1935. Today, the growing support of the medical profession for assisted dying will eventually help to change the law.

- The above is an extract from a series of factsheets on euthanasia issues, produced by the Voluntary Eu-thanasia Society. See page 41 for address details.

© *Voluntary Euthanasia Society, 1998*

Helping hand?

Physician-assisted suicide stirs strong emotions. Doctors have called for a conference in the hope of reaching a consensus

In ancient Greece, if a person could convince the Senate they had good reasons for ending their life, they were given a free prescription of hemlock. Few societies since have taken quite such a lenient view towards assisting suicide.

In Britain, while it is no longer illegal to attempt suicide, assisting suicide is a criminal offence. In some circumstances it may constitute murder. Doctors, even if they consider themselves to be acting in the best interests of a patient, are not exempt from the law.

To some doctors, the idea of assisting a patient in ending their life is repugnant. They would agree with Kent GP Anne Rodway, former deputy chairman of the BMA medical ethics committee, when she says: 'I want patients to know that I have a licence to heal and not a licence to kill.'

Others are not so sure. After years of opposition to physician-assisted suicide (PAS), doctors at this year's BMA annual representative meeting called for a conference on the issue.

But what is meant by PAS? In the American state of Oregon, where PAS has been legalised, it is understood to mean that a doctor, following a request from a patient, gives the patient the medication to end his or her life. This is different from euthanasia, where the doctor administers the lethal drugs.

Different again are cases of withdrawing and withholding treatment, like that of Hillsborough disaster victim Tony Bland. In 1993 the House of Lords allowed doctors to withhold nutrition from a patient in a persistent vegetative state even though it would lead to death.

The Law Lords distinguished between the illegal act of deliberately causing death, as in euthanasia, and the omission of life-preserving treatment that is considered clinically futile.

Individual cases do not always fall into these neat categories. And campaigners both for and against PAS tend to lump it together with other end-of-life issues because they want to show the moral similarities between them.

When PAS was sanctioned in Oregon last year, many supporters carried placards with just three words upon them: Right to Die. Their argument is that PAS is a matter of patient autonomy, that patients should be able to choose to die as they can choose other treatments and doctors should respect their wishes.

Voluntary Euthanasia Society chairman and former GP Michael Irwin says: 'We may be uncomfortable with the thought but there are patients who, after considering the options open to them in terms of palliative care, want to die. Doctors have the responsibility of giving patients the fullest possible picture of their diagnosis and prognosis so they can reach an informed decision.'

Professor of law and ethics in medicine at Glasgow University Sheila McLean agrees. In her book *Sometimes a Small Victory*, she writes: 'It is the patient who must make a choice of whether they wish to die or not, and the proper role of the physician would be to facilitate that choice through effective communication skills.'

Sacred

This argument is rejected by former Liverpool GP Peggy Norris, chairman of the pressure group Alert, which opposes what it sees as medically sanctioned killing. Dr Norris reveals that her late husband James, a GP, was sent home from hospital to die with stomach cancer in 1974, but lived for a further 11 years.

She says: 'As a doctor and a Roman Catholic, I see life as sacred. It is not the patient's or the doctor's job to decide whether it should be taken away. This is simply not an option.'

But, as in the Bland case, society has already accepted that life should not always be preserved at all costs.

Anglican bishops at last month's Lambeth Conference agreed. While opposing both PAS and euthanasia, they said withdrawing and withholding treatments from patients in a persistent vegetative state could enable a 'dignified' death in keeping with Christian teaching.

The argument is not about the patient's right to die, but the doctor's duty to help them with it. Dr Irwin questions whether there is a distinction between a doctor who, after judging a patient to be terminally ill and in great pain, provides the means to commit suicide, and another who gives such a high dose of a pain-relieving drug that it may prove fatal.

The former is PAS and is illegal. The latter is legal under the principle of double effect, where providing a doctor's primary aim is to relieve pain, a treatment can allowably have the side-effect of hastening death. Dr Irwin says some doctors use the double effect to help patients die.

Finding evidence on this is difficult. Ask doctors whether their primary objective is to relieve pain or to cause death and they will say the former.

One Manchester GP, who did not want to be named, says: 'I had an elderly patient with a very advanced form of cancer and she begged me to help her die. She said that if she had the strength to reach the bleach in her kitchen cupboard she would have drunk it.

'I'm not saying I helped her die. But I prescribed medication in such a dose that it probably relieved a great deal of pain and at the same time gave a higher risk of causing death. She died a couple of days later.'

Dr Irwin argues it would be better to have a system where doctors can collaborate with patients more openly about ending their lives and within a regulatory framework.

One of the arguments in favour of PAS is that it would allow the process to be regulated. But would it be possible to design a system of regulation that prevented abuses? Lawyer and former chairman of the civil rights group Liberty Malcolm Hurwitt points to the example of Oregon, where the first death under the Death with Dignity Act took place earlier this year. He says: 'It is too early to say whether the law in Oregon offers all the safeguards necessary, but it would make a good starting point for legislation in Britain.'

Possible abuses

In Oregon, the law states that patients will only be assisted with their suicide if they are terminally ill and likely to die within six months,

have been informed of their diagnosis and prognosis, and have been offered the alternatives in palliative care.

But reader in healthcare law at Southampton University Jonathan Montgomery is not so confident. Mr Montgomery, who teaches medical ethics and wrote the influential text book *Health Care Law*, supports the philosophical arguments for PAS but he has yet to hear of a system that could counter all the possible abuses. Patients could be harangued by relatives who stood to gain financially from their death, they could change their minds when it was too late, or choose death because they had not been fully informed about the alternatives, to list just a few.

Mr Montgomery says: 'The way I usually teach students is by asking them which mistakes they find more palatable – mistakes that keep people alive or mistakes that cause them to die. I prefer to keep them alive.'

Patients' Association chairman Claire Rayner, speaking personally, agrees. 'The risk of the system being abused is just too great to change the law.

To Dorset palliative care consultant Fiona Randall, however, all talk of abuses and safeguards is irrelevant. She says that to offer assistance with suicide to any section of the population is both morally wrong and hypocritical.

Dr Randall, a former BMA medical ethics committee deputy chairman, says: 'One of the government's targets is reducing suicide. Against that background, is it really logical to encourage and assist people who are sick to commit suicide?

'PAS does not reinforce the idea that we are personally of value. It would give out the message "If you are sick, doctors will help you kill yourselves. You are not of value."'

Consensus on PAS seems a long way off. It remains an issue where the profession is split down the middle.

BMA medical ethics committee chairman Michael Wilks says: 'I welcome the idea of having a conference. It would be ambitious to imagine consensus would arise from a single conference but it may be a way to start the process.'

A *News Review* survey of 750 doctors in 1996 found 32 per cent would supply drugs to a terminally ill patient to assist suicide, 52 per cent would not and 16 per cent were undecided.

'I'll carry on within the bounds of what I can do legally,' says the Manchester GP.

'Sometimes the way I treat dying patients makes me feel shoddy, guilty and a little bit pointless. But I've yet to find a better alternative.'

© *BMA News Review*
September, 1998

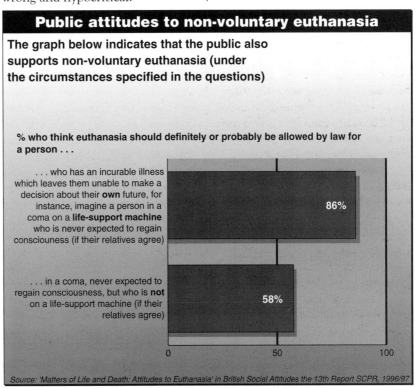

Public attitudes to non-voluntary euthanasia

The graph below indicates that the public also supports non-voluntary euthanasia (under the circumstances specified in the questions)

% who think euthanasia should definitely or probably be allowed by law for a person . . .

. . . who has an incurable illness which leaves them unable to make a decision about their **own** future, for instance, imagine a person in a coma on a **life-support machine** who is never expected to regain consciousness (if their relatives agree) — **86%**

. . . in a coma, never expected to regain consciousness, but who is **not** on a life-support machine (if their relatives agree) — **58%**

Source: 'Matters of Life and Death: Attitudes to Euthanasia' in British Social Attitudes the 13th Report SCPR, 1996/97

Euthanasia – should we let courts decide?

Catholic doctors were split this week over the best way to stop euthanasia becoming law after a new document by two influential Catholic bodies stopped short of recommending an outright ban on withdrawing food and fluid from seriously ill patients.

The 17-page document, drawn up by the Guild of Catholic Doctors and the Catholic Union of Great Britain, said withholding nutrition was 'intrinsically wrong' but still accepted that grave decisions should be tackled by the courts.

The Joint Ethico Medical Committee, the body that produced the new paper, admitted that its stance could be seen as a climbdown by some Catholics but insisted that court intervention was preferable to allowing health professionals or families alone to make difficult life and death decisions.

But Dr Peggy Norris, chair of the anti-euthanasia group, ALERT, said she did not believe that decisions over the withdrawal of assisted nutrition were best dealt with by the courts in the light of the Tony Bland judgement.

In 1993 a court ruled that Tony Bland who had been in a persistent vegetative state (PVS) since the 1989 Hillsborough disaster, should be 'allowed to die' by withdrawing his artificial feeding tube.

Catholic doctors' groups believe that the landmark decision changed the homicide law, altering the common law requirement to provide basic nourishment to patients.

'Providing food and fluid is part of basic nursing care. It does not constitute medical treatment. But the Tony Bland decision confused everything,' said Dr Norris.

'When I was a medical student, we were taught to recognise when a patient was dying. It was never considered right to prolong the dying process.

'If you realise your patient is

dying you don't pump food and fluid into them.

'That is the distinction between someone who is dying and someone who is incapacitated and still very much alive. You don't have to go to court to make these decisions.'

Dr Tony Cole, chairman of the Joint Ethico Medical Committee, said that Catholic doctors faced the problem of dealing with a medical community which does not share its views on most moral and ethical decisions.

He told the *Catholic Times*: 'If we can't get across our whole point, we need a fall back point. We have to accept that this can't be an ideal situation.

'In *Evangelium Vitae*, the Pope makes exactly this point. He says we must strive to put the Catholic viewpoint as best as possible.

'All our information is made available to the bishops and we do our best to stay within Catholic teaching.'

Persistent vegetative state is a condition that is little understood

---

Dr Cole said the 15-strong committee made up of doctors, lawyers, a theologian and Catholics with a background in the civil service and Department of Health, was now convinced it had enough medical evidence to prove its case in any court action on food and fluid withdrawal.

'Our understanding of how people suffer from thirst has advanced. We would hope that we could persuade a court that withholding hydration or nutrition is not an acceptable course of action.

'The Guild is now able to put forward a lot of evidence to the official solicitor. Persistent vegetative state is a condition that is little understood. We are trying to increase understanding in this area.'

But the *Catholic Times* understands that some Catholic doctors are still concerned that courts will still find in favour of allowing the withdrawal of food and fluids.

Dr Michael Jarmulowicz, secretary of the Guild of Catholic Doctors, but not a member of the Joint Ethico Medical Committee, said: 'There is a danger with lawyers who are pro-euthanasia. I think that the Official Solicitor is quite happy with withdrawing food and fluids.'

© *The Catholic Times*
November, 1998

Kill or cure is not a choice for doctors

By Tom Utley

Many years ago, a doctor friend, who was then the consultant in charge of the intensive therapy unit at a teaching hospital, told me a story that shocked me profoundly. It was at the time of an NHS pay dispute, and my friend was having trouble with the sister responsible for the nurses in his unit, whom he described as a formidable and uncooperative woman at the best of times.

A couple of days earlier, said my friend, a patient had been brought into the casualty department at his hospital, suffering from severe head injuries after a car crash. My friend told the sister to admit the patient immediately to the ITU – but she refused, saying that there was no bed for him. My friend pointed to one of the empty beds in the unit and said: 'Put him in that one.' But still the sister refused. For when nursing sisters speak of hospital beds, they do not mean the things that patients lie in; they mean the team of nurses available to minister to each patient. If I remember rightly, the rule at the time was that there should be a rota of four nurses for every patient in the ITU.

My friend was exasperated. He told the sister that, unless she admitted the patient to the unit immediately, he was going to die. The sister remained unmoved. My friend lost his temper, strode over to one of the beds where another patient was lying in a coma and put his finger on the switch of his life-support machine. He then turned to the sister and said: 'If you do not put the patient from casualty in that empty bed, I am going to switch off this machine and you can put him in this one.'

The sister put her hands on her hips and said: 'Go on, then. Do it.' And here comes the bit that shocked me: he *did*. Rather than lose face in front of the other nurses on the ward, he deliberately ended the life of one of his patients.

That was how my friend put it to me, anyway, although he back-tracked frantically when he saw the colour draining from my cheeks and realised how horrified I was. The patient whose death he had hastened was as good as dead in any case, he said, and he had already considered switching off the life-support machine earlier that day. His decision had given the car-crash victim his only chance of survival – although he, too, had later died. Perhaps, said my friend, he had embellished the story a little, but it was essentially true. What surprised him was that I had been so terribly shocked. It was not a particularly remarkable incident, he thought. He had to make decisions about whether his patients should live or die almost every day of his working week.

My friend's explanation pacified me a little and I stopped thinking that perhaps I ought to report him to the police. I reflected that it was probably priggish of me, as a layman, to see his story starkly in terms of right and wrong. I could see that, for doctors with day-to-day responsibilities like his, the moral edges were bound to become a little blurred. Very often they hasten their patients' deaths by withdrawing treatment that has become futile, in that it is doing no more than prolonging the process of dying. Occasionally, too, they may hasten death by prescribing dangerously high doses of painkillers to the terminally ill. I see no strong objection to this, as long as the doctor's primary purpose in prescribing these is to ease pain.

There is a world of difference, however, between hastening death in these ways and setting out deliberately to kill patients, as Dr Jack Kevorkian has done in America.

And here I remain a moral absolutist. I find Dr Kevorkian's behaviour disgusting, exhibitionist and deeply wrong. His decision to film himself 'assisting the suicide' of Thomas Youk for prime-time television was the act of a pornographer, not of a doctor. I am delighted that the state of Michigan has granted his wish that he should be prosecuted, and I hope that he is sent to rot in jail.

It would be tempting to dismiss Dr Kevorkian's activities as the sort of thing that could happen only in America. But the euthanasia lobby is gathering strength in Britain. Even the charity Age Concern, which one might think would have more respect for the lives of the elderly, has published arguments in its favour in its 'Millennium Paper', *Values and Attitudes in an Ageing Society*. The threat of a law to legalise euthanasia and assisted suicides has become so real that, last month, a group of doctors formed to campaign against it. They chose the name First Do No Harm – a Hippocratic injunction.

Some members of the group believe that, if euthanasia is legalised, it may become common practice, to bump off the elderly. If that sounds alarmist, one need only consider the spread of abortion since it became legal. Introduced to product women whose health would be endangered

---

'I never want to have to wonder whether the physician coming into my hospital room is wearing the white coat of the healer . . . or the black hood of the executioner. The words of an American lawyer, Alexander Capron.

---

by childbirth, it is now a common form of birth control. More than any other, the abortion law undermined the principle that human life is sacred, and set everybody quibbling instead about how to define life. In that sense, it prepared the way for the euthanasia lobby.

I know that it is easy for me, as a healthy, middle-aged man suffering no pain, to affirm that human life is sacred and that abortion, euthanasia and suicide are wrong. But sacrifice that principle, it seems to me, and the entire moral universe collapses.

The guidelines on euthanasia issued by the British Medical Association, which strongly opposes it, are a model of humanity and good

sense. They say that, even if euthanasia does become legal, doctors should have nothing to do with it, quoting approvingly the words of an American lawyer, Alexander Capron: 'I never want to have to wonder whether the physician coming into my hospital room is wearing the white coat of the healer . . . or the black hood of the executioner. Trust between patient and physician is simply too important and too fragile to be subjected to the unnecessary strain.' That should be every British doctor's answer to Dr Kevorkian.

I have one footnote to add to my doctor friend's story. Last week, I met a former nurse who had worked with him in his ITU. Unprompted, she told me that he was the most brilliant physician with whom she had ever worked, with an astonishing instinct for knowing where there was hope and where there was none. She said that countless patients owed their lives to his instinct and to his refusal to give up, when everybody else thought the case hopeless. I am now sure that I would trust my friend with the decision about whether to switch off my life-support machine. I just hope that, if he *does* switch it off, he will refrain from regaling the company with it at dinner parties.

Doctor, will you help me die?

A new study shows many family doctors secretly hasten the deaths of terminally ill patients, and many more think they should be able to do so legally. Cherry Norton reports on the dilemmas of euthanasia

Nobody can deny the courage of Jennifer Lyle-Purdy as she faces up to the greatest of decisions. A former fashion buyer for a large company, Lyle-Purdy, 66, has multiple sclerosis, a debilitating condition that gradually leads to paralysis.

There is no cure for the disease, which affects about 85,000 people in Britain, but Lyle-Purdy is determined that it will be she who has the final say in her life, not the illness.

A year after being told she had MS Lyle-Purdy was also diagnosed

with cancer and doctors said she had only a 50% chance of survival. She beat the cancer, but the experience brought her face to face with her mortality.

'I do not want to be left lingering in agony,' she said. 'There is no way that any human being should have to suffer when death is inevitable.'

So she has chosen to draw up a living will – a form setting out how she wishes to die – which she has lodged with her GP and two hospitals. She has no desire to end her life at present, but her living will

requests that she be given a lethal injection when she becomes helpless and the pain becomes unbearable.

'I found it empowering to say what I wanted to happen to me,' she said. 'It has given me peace of mind.'

However, any doctor who accedes to her wishes and assists in her death runs the risk of committing a serious crime. Euthanasia or assisted suicide, no matter how well intentioned or dignified, is illegal in Britain. Perpetrators can be charged with murder.

Lyle-Purdy is not too worried

that she will be left with nobody to help her. Euthanasia may be illegal but it happens all the time.

A study of 300 GPs has revealed that one in seven admits to helping patients die at their request. It indicates that hundreds, probably thousands, of patients die each year with the help of doctors at home, in hospices and in hospital. Even more GPs, though they may not admit to helping patients die, believe it would be right for doctors to be given the legal power of death.

Some 68% of doctors who replied to a confidential questionnaire from the *Sunday Times* said that a doctor should be able to assist death by withdrawing or withholding treatment – without fear of prosecution. And 60% believe that they should be able to administer large doses of painkillers in the full knowledge that this is likely to shorten life.

A smaller number, 18%, even believe doctors should be able to prescribe lethal medication that patients can take with the intention of killing themselves.

One of the 'defining moments' in the career of Dr Nigel Scott-Moncrieff, a GP in London, came when he was a young houseman. A man was brought into hospital suffering from severe cardiac failure, a condition where the heart cannot pump blood around the body and the lungs fill with fluid. 'Patients die from drowning in their own juices,' he said.

Under the supervision of a consultant, who knew the patient and his family, Scott-Moncrieff strove to relieve the man's suffering. 'I tried several drugs to off-load the fluid from his lungs and eventually switched to diamorphine to relieve the pain,' he recalled.

The battle went on for hours and Scott-Moncrieff regularly conferred by telephone with the consultant, discussing the dosage to administer. At one point, recalled Scott-Moncrieff, 'the consultant said to me: "Do you think that [the dosage] will work?" So I increased it and the man died soon after the injection.'

When Scott-Moncrieff called the consultant to tell him the patient had died, he replied: 'You are learning.'

It is a lesson Scott-Moncrieff has not forgotten; in his career he has assisted in the deaths of at least two people at their request and eased the passing of others.

The commonest way doctors hasten death is by injecting large doses of diamorphine, another name for heroin. It is sometimes mixed with barbiturates. The ostensible and entirely legal purpose is to alleviate pain. But the result of high dosages can also be death.

The patient does not die immediately but slips into unconsciousness and passes away within hours as the drug suppresses breathing.

'Diamorphine is the ultimate painkiller. It detaches someone completely from the pain and the fear of death. It is the most delightful and delicious way to die,' Scott-Moncrieff said.

It is a common enough occurrence, according to Dr Christopher Hindley, a London GP who has assisted up to 10 patients to die at their request. Many GPs, he says, deploy this doctrine of 'double effect': they legitimately use drugs to lessen

---

'I do not want to be left lingering in agony. There is no way that any human being should have to suffer when death is inevitable'

---

pain knowing the result will be death. But it is, he says, hypocritical because 'the intention is to shorten life'.

To make matters more complicated, Hindley says that requests from patients for help with suicide are often less than explicit. 'A lot is non-verbal, often patients are so weak they cannot express themselves clearly,' he said. 'It does not have to be a formal request of "I want out", but a hint of "can't we speed things up?" Usually it happens when the relative or nurse is out of the room and there is that quiet conversation.'

A 45-year-old doctor from Bristol, who did not want to be named, said that he had assisted the deaths of five patients at their request. 'I have watched two patients die from terminal incurable diseases. It was awful,' he said. 'A vet would have had no hesitation in "putting them to sleep", and neither would the families concerned.'

Another doctor, who has also helped five patients to die, said there were many cases where the family of a patient helped. He would visit someone's house to prescribe painkillers and if the patient was in severe pain and close to death, tell the family: 'Be very careful to give only two tablets as another two would probably make him pass away.'

The doctor, from north London, said: 'And I know full well that before I have gone round the corner they will have given him that extra dose.'

The dangers of unbridled euthanasia are all too easy to imagine. In an extraordinary account of falling into a coma after an accident, Joan Smith (not her real name), a 42-year-old businesswoman, recently described how she was completely paralysed but could hear everything happening around her.

'I could hear the doctors discussing me, so I knew how ill I was. I heard them saying that my lungs were full of poison and there wasn't much hope. Twice a priest came into the room and gave me the last rites,' she said.

Smith, who was put on a respirator, was shocked when she heard her husband tell doctors that she would not have wanted to live in such circumstances and they should switch off the respirator. 'My husband was issuing my death sentence – I wanted to scream,' she said, but she was unable to move. Thanks only to the persistence of her daughter, her treatment was continued and she eventually made a full recovery.

Nevertheless, the pressure for a change to the strict illegality of euthanasia is growing, with calls for more formal guidance on what doctors can and cannot do. The law is inexorably being drawn into the debate.

In June, Gillian Jennison, a lecturer at Bradford University, faced trial after admitting she had helped her mother to commit suicide. Jennison had given her 82-year-old mother, who was suffering from chronic dementia, sleeping pills and then smothered her with a pillow.

The judge told Jennison that it was only the exceptional circumstances of the case that prevented her from facing a murder charge. Instead she pleaded guilty to aiding and abetting suicide and was sentenced to probation. The judge declared that he was satisfied that 'what was done was in the honest belief that it was what your mother wanted'.

By contrast, when Jeremy Beadle, the television presenter, recently admitted helping a friend to die, and when others have spoken in a similar vein, no action has been taken.

Zoe Wanamaker, the actress, has also spoken out in favour of euthanasia. She considered helping her father to die, but in the end took no action.

The British Medical Association remains opposed to any change in the law on euthanasia and doctor-assisted suicide. But it has had to respond to the views of a substantial number of doctors who want to clarify when they should allow patients to die.

This week the BMA held a meeting to discuss results of its own survey on the subject. It intends to draw up national guidelines to help doctors decide when sustaining treatment of a patient is 'in-appropriate even though it is technically feasible'.

Lord Irvine of Lairg, the Lord Chancellor, published a green paper last year seeking views on whether the law governing living wills should be changed. At present living wills have only limited legal standing. But in the *Sunday Times* study, a majority of GPs support the idea of living wills; 69% said they were a good idea and 44% thought they should have more legal force. Almost one in five thought living wills should also be legally enforceable for children.

Yet in the countries that have tried to legislate on people's right to die, the results are mixed. Since 1993 doctors in Holland have been able to stop the suffering of terminally ill patients and end their lives with or without their consent. Each year 25,000 Dutch people die this way.

More than 10,000 Dutch people, however, now carry anti-euthanasia cards because they are concerned that if they fall ill they will be killed off prematurely by overzealous doctors.

In the Northern Territory, Australia, a law to enable the terminally ill to have legal assistance in committing suicide was soon overturned.

To Scott-Moncrieff, the law will never be the answer to the ethical dilemmas of euthanasia. The only practical approach, he believes, is to address the merits of each individual case – and that is one of the roles of doctors. There are no hard-and-fast rules and it is better to keep the law out of it.

He recalled attending a doctor who knew he was dying from severe cardiac failure. Fluid was blowing up his body like a balloon.

The doctor said to Scott-Moncrieff: 'I don't know you very well, but I trust you. I am going to die soon. I know it, my family know it and my children know it. I think you know what to do.'

To Scott-Moncrieff, the doctor was asking him to make sure he did not suffer. When the time came he injected the patient with a large dose of diamorphine; death followed within an hour.

'I cannot understand doctors who want to legalise it [euthanasia],' he said. 'There is no need to, The fact is, this is the way medicine has run since time began.'

Doctor knows best?

Have you ever been asked by a patient to help them die?
44% Yes   56% No

Have you ever assisted a patient's death at their request?
15% Yes   83% No

Do you think doctors should have the power to assist death without fear of prosecution:
a) by withholding treatment?
68% Yes   31% No

b) by withdrawing treatment?
67% Yes   32% No

c) by administering painkillers in the knowledge that they are likely to shorten life?
60% Yes   37% No

d) by prescribing lethal drugs for patients to take themselves?
18% Yes   75% No

Do you believe in a patient's right to die?
63% Yes   33% No

Do you think it is a good idea for patients to make living wills?
69% Yes   27% No

Figures may not add up to 100 because not all doctors answered all questions.

Psychiatrists' attitudes

National survey of UK psychiatrists' attitudes to euthanasia

Opinion is moving toward the toleration, or even legalisation, of assisted suicide.[1] During the short time assisted suicide was decriminalised in the Northern Territory, Australia, a psychiatric assessment of candidates was obligatory, although few psychiatrists were willing to take part in such assessment. The draft bill for the legalisation of physician-assisted suicide presented to the UK Parliament in 1997 did not include provision for assessment by a psychiatrist. However, psychiatric illness could preclude a valid request for assisted suicide and psychiatrists are perceived to be well placed to assess suicidal intent and diagnose mental illness. Psychiatrists in the UK have not been consulted about their views on assisted suicide. The only surveys of this type have been in the Netherlands, USA, and Australia, where assisted suicide has been legally sanctioned.[2]

We investigated psychiatrists' opinions before any changes in legislation in the UK. A 20-item questionnaire was devised with a selection of items derived from other questionnaires previously distributed to physicians in the USA.[3,4] Statements were placed beside a five-point Likert scale that ranged from strongly agree to strongly disagree. We sought information on views of assisted suicide and on the related issues of passive euthanasia and voluntary active euthanasia. We then asked about safeguards deemed necessary if assisted suicide were to be made legitimate and on the role of the psychiatrist.

The questionnaire was sent to 538 senior psychiatrists selected randomly from the Royal College of Psychiatrists' mailing list by a computer algorithm, and was re-mailed 6 weeks later. 88 questionnaires were returned undelivered. Of the remaining 450 questionnaires, 322 (72%) were completed and returned. The mean age of the

By Nisha Shah, James Warner, Bob Blizard, Michael King

respondents was 47 (range 31 to 76 years), and 206 (64%) were men. To facilitate presentation, the Likert scale responses were reclassified into three groups: agree, neutral, and disagree. Data were summarised by Statistical Package for Social Science. The questions about psychiatrists' attitudes to assisted suicide and their role in the assessment process are shown in the table.

The high response rate from this postal survey indicates the level of interest among UK psychiatrists. Widespread agreement that so-called rational suicide exists is interesting since most suicides are said to occur in the context of mental illness.[5] This view suggests that not all suicides are a result of mental illness. Voluntary active euthanasia was more strongly rejected than passive euthanasia; the closer the involvement of the physician, the less the support for assistance in dying. Similarly, although most agreed that psychiatric assessment should be obligatory in any patient who requests assisted suicide, few were prepared to carry this out personally.

This is the first survey of psychiatrists' attitudes to assisted suicide in the UK. Most psychiatrists believe that suicide may be a rational act, and accept passive euthanasia. However, many are unwilling to use their skills to exclude mental illness in people who request assisted suicide.

1 Josefson D. United States sees first legal euthanasia case. *BMJ* 1998; 316: 1037.

2 Roberts LW, Muskin PR, Warner TD, et al. Attitudes of consultation-liaison psychiatrists toward physician-assisted death practices. *Psychosomatics* 1997; 38: 459-71.

3 Cohen JS, Fihn SD, Boyko EJ, Jonsen AR, Wood RW. Attitudes toward assisted suicide and euthanasia among physicians in Washington State. *N Engl J Med* 1994; 331: 89-94.

4 Doukas D, Waterhouse D, Gorenflo DW, Seid J. Attitudes and behaviours on physician-assisted death: a study of Michigan oncologists. *J Clin Oncol* 1995; 13: 1055-61.

5 Barraclough B, Bunch J, Nelson B, Sainsbury P. A hundred cases of suicide: clinical aspects. *Br J Psychiatry* 1974; 125: 355-73.

© The Lancet
October, 1998

Backing for passive euthanasia

Most psychiatrists support the idea of passive euthanasia and believe suicide does not depend on mental illness, according to a survey undertaken by the Royal Free Hospital, London. A total of 538 senior psychiatrists were sent a questionnaire, and 322 responded.

Statement on questionnaire	Strongly agree/agree	Neutral	Disagree/ strongly disagree
Assisted suicide should be legal	38	18	44
Suicide may be rational	86	7	7
Passive euthanasia not justifiable	9	8	83
Assisted suicide not justifiable	43	17	40
Voluntary active euthanasia not justifiable	50	21	29
Psychiatric assessment in all cases	64	13	23
Willing to assess psychological suitability	35	18	47
Non-comptetent patients should be eligible for assisted suicide if advance directive exists	36	23	40
Willing to assist suicide	20	17	63

Passive euthanasia = withholding or withdrawing of life-sustaining medical treatment; assisted suicide = intentional provision of the instruction or the means by which a person may kill him/herself; voluntary active euthanasia = active intervention by a doctor to end life at request of recipient.

Source: The Lancet

Fighting to die with dignity

As the heated euthanasia debate reaches fever pitch, Janet Snell describes one terminally ill nurse's fight for the right to die with dignity

As a student nurse, Jane Macdonald was asked to assist a qualified member of staff in giving morphine to an unconscious elderly female patient.

'Of course, it hastened the woman's death, but she was very sick and everyone thought it for the best. I know that sort of thing still happens, but what I want to see is the whole issue brought out in the open. It shouldn't be the doctors, or even the family, who decide, it should be the patient. And a dignified death through euthanasia ought to be one option open to them.'

Jane is now a campaigner for the Voluntary Euthanasia Society, but like so many other members, her involvement with the organisation only began after she herself became ill.

She has multiple sclerosis and had a mastectomy in 1994 following a diagnosis of breast cancer. Now, at the age of 49, she has discovered she has bone secondaries.

'They've also told me I have osteoporosis, which just about puts the icing on the cake,' she adds wryly. 'People say to me don't you ever feel "why me?" But my response is "why not me?" They tell me I'm brave, but there's nothing brave in getting on with your life. What else can you do but try and keep smiling and enjoying what time you have left?'

Jane believes her nursing background has helped her come to terms with serious illness. 'I think one thing it's really taught me is not to be afraid of my own body. That may sound odd, but there are lots of pretty filthy things I have to do for myself, like intermittent catheterisation. Now I know from talking to non-nursing friends with MS that they are horrified at the thought of such a thing. But as a nurse you take it in your stride.'

Jane trained at Westminster Hospital in London and went on to be a staff nurse at Roehampton in Surrey. But her father, an army brigadier, had other ideas.

'He wasn't happy with what I was paid, so he would send me application forms for joining the army nurses as they were generally much better paid. I received one when I was feeling particularly exhausted by our fight to keep the casualty department open and I sent off the application.'

That led to eight happy years in the Queen Alexandra Army Nursing Corps, where she trained as an RMN and took a tutor's diploma. She only left so she could stay in the country after meeting her future husband Jonathan.

Jane took a job at the RCN as student officer, later moving to the UKCC as a professional officer.

'I had been having symptoms for some time – dragging my leg and so on – and I thought I'd better go and get a diagnosis before my colleagues started looking for gin bottles under my desk. So I went to see a neurologist, had a scan and he told me I had MS. I suspected I might because my sister has it, which made my diagnosis all the more devastating for my parents. But at least it wasn't a brain tumour.'

Jane did not realise the illness would eventually force her to give up her job. 'I'd probably nursed about 12 or 14 people at the final stages of MS, but for some reason I just didn't think what happened to them would happen to me. The first thing I did when I got the diagnosis was to go off and do an MBA, partly because I wanted to see if my brain was still functioning, and partly because I wanted other people to see my brain was still functioning.'

Eventually she became too ill to go to work and diverted what energy she did have into lobbying on behalf of the Voluntary Euthanasia Society. She became good friends with Annie Lindsell, another prominent society member who died last December after a long battle with motor neurone disease.

'Before Annie died we were talking, and she said: "What's going to happen to the campaign when there's none of us left?" She joked that it was like that song about 10 green bottles and there needed to be a replacement after each of us fell.

'It's important for the media to have people like us who are facing death to talk about euthanasia as it makes the message much more potent.'

When Jane is well enough she speaks at conferences and attends meetings on euthanasia, assisted by Lennie, her Labrador/Retriever, who walks in a rigid harness which supports her. 'It's partly thanks to Lennie that I still have a reasonable degree of independence. Life's not so bad, and the only thing I fear is loss of dignity at the end, which is why I'm campaigning. This green bottle will eventually fall, but I know there will always be another ready to get up there and carry on the fight.'

Reproduced by kind permission of Nursing Times where this article first appeared on 18 November, 1998

Dutch carry card that says: Don't kill me, doctor

By Rachel Bridge

More than 10,000 people in Holland have started carrying anti-euthanasia 'passports' because they are frightened of being killed prematurely by over-enthusiastic doctors if they fall ill.

The move comes as the newly-elected Dutch government presses ahead with a proposal to legalise 'assisted suicide' by doctors, the first of its kind in Europe.

The Bill is being pushed through despite the government's own surveys showing that Dutch doctors are increasingly practising non-voluntary euthanasia and are ending patients' lives without their approval. It is estimated that every year up to 25,000 people die when their treatment is terminated on medical grounds.

According to the most recent survey into euthanasia – carried out in 1995 and sponsored by the Dutch government – 23 per cent of doctors said that they had ended a patient's life without his or her explicit request.

Although euthanasia is technically illegal in Holland, doctors who assist with voluntary euthanasia rarely face prosecution. As a consequence an estimated 3,000 patients die each year after they have specifically requested that their lives be terminated.

The 'declaration of life' cards, which are being distributed by pro-life groups throughout Holland, carry the words: 'I request that no medical treatment be withheld on the grounds that the future quality of my life will be diminished, because I believe that this is not something that human beings can judge. I request that under no circumstances a life-ending treatment be administered because I am of the opinion that people do not have the right to end life.'

Opponents are concerned that enshrining voluntary euthanasia into law will turn assisted suicide into a fully accepted medical practice. In particular they fear that it will encourage doctors to carry out euthanasia without prior consultation. But supporters of the law say that it will bring all assisted suicides under closer scrutiny.

Under current guidelines, a doctor is required to report all cases of euthanasia to the public prosecutor. But many do not comply, partly because of the stigma of reporting to the public prosecutor's office, but also because they run the risk of prosecution if they are judged to have wrongly applied the euthanasia process.

From next month, however, doctors will report to an advisory committee, comprising medical, ethical and legal experts. Only if the committee is dissatisfied will a case be referred to the prosecutor.

'This is awful,' said Dr Peggy Norris, the chairman of the World Federation of Doctors Who Respect Human Life. 'It is the most vulnerable who will be affected. There will be added pressure on patients to think that they are a nuisance to their family and that perhaps it is better to

ask the doctor for something and die now rather than later.' Helen Watt, a research fellow at the Roman Catholic Church-backed Linacre Centre of Healthcare Ethics in London, said: 'If something is legally tolerated then people tend to assume it is right. It becomes part of the medical culture.' While the majority of doctors and public opinion in Holland support the practice of voluntary euthanasia, there is growing concern that assisted suicide is increasingly dominating medical practice to the exclusion of other treatments.

The Dutch Physicians' Association said that doctors who oppose voluntary euthanasia were frightened to speak out for fear of losing their jobs. The association, whose predominately Christian membership is against the practice of voluntary euthanasia, has begun telling its 500 members not to mention their views when applying for a job.

Dr Krijn Haasnood, the association's spokesman, said: 'There is much pressure on doctors to practise euthanasia. Up to now a doctor who did not want to carry out euthanasia could say that it was against the law, but now it will be the right of the patient to request it. It will be part of the job of the doctor. We are going into a new area and we don't know where it will end. It is a total change in the role of the doctor if killing patients becomes part of the job.'

Anneke Verhoeven, a spokesman for the Lifewish Declaration Foundation, part of the Dutch Patients' Association, which produces one of the anti-euthanasia passports, said: 'When you are ill, euthanasia seems to be a solution but it is not. There is so much that can be done to ease pain and suffering. Sometimes people too quickly think that the pain is unbearable and that life is no longer worth living.'

BMA moves on suicide

Doctors to hold conference on assisted deaths

By Sarah Boseley,
Health Correspondent

Doctors, uneasy at what they see as efforts by the pro-euthanasia lobby to enlist them in their cause, are to call a major conference to discuss whether they should help very sick patients to commit suicide.

The issue sparked a tense debate at the British Medical Association's annual meeting in Cardiff yesterday. The BMA's official position is opposed to euthanasia and physician-assisted suicide, which are both illegal. But those who feel that doctors must discuss the difficult ethical issues further and establish the views if possible of all healthcare professionals, led by a contingent of junior doctors, won the day.

John Marks, former BMA chairman, made an impassioned call for representatives to listen to the voice of youth, reminding them of a previous ethical dilemma. 'In 1968, the policy of this association was that although so-called social abortion was legal, it was unethical. I told the meeting they were hypocritical, not Hippocratical, because any patient of mine with £100 in her pocket could get an abortion.' He had been booed off the platform, he said, and yet four years later, David Steel's Abortion Bill went through.

'In over 40 years, I have never deliberately killed a patient, but I have given them increasing doses, sometimes huge doses, of drugs to ease their pain in their final weeks, knowing that it might shorten their lives. Perhaps I'm being hypocritical, I don't know. I just know that when the time comes, I want a doctor who will give me a lot of assistance.

'It is just possible that the young Turks are light years ahead of the fuddy-duddies, as they were 30 years ago, but only full and open discussion can tell us,' he said.

Carl Erhardt, a senior registrar at Charing Cross hospital in London, said a conference was 'quite unnecessary'. Physician-assisted suicide was 'not only morally wrong but quite incompatible with the ethics of medicine'. He observed that 'the right to die organisations in the UK appear to be increasingly focusing on assisted suicide as a first stage in achieving their aim of euthanasia.'

He also referred to doctors in the Netherlands who had controversially helped patients to die. 'I understand that the Dutch experience shows that euthanasia, once sanctioned, is applied to those who have not asked for it.'

But Stuart Horner, a former chairman of the BMA's ethics committee, said he 'shared the concern of those who fear that the protagonists of euthanasia, having so spectacularly failed in an open agenda, are now resorting by stealth to a hidden agenda.

'Decisions at the end of life are becoming increasingly part of modern medical practice. They will not go away because we refuse to discuss them.'

The meeting overwhelmingly voted for the proposed conference to try to find a common position, even though most speakers made it clear that they did not expect the BMA's opposition to physician-assisted suicide to change.

But a motion declaring that doctors had an obligation to their patients to help them end their lives,

> **'Decisions at the end of life are becoming increasingly part of modern medical practice. They will not go away because we refuse to discuss them'**

if that was what they wanted, was soundly defeated.

At a press conference afterwards, Michael Wilks, chairman of the ethics committee, said more patients were not asking doctors to help them die. It was not something patients wanted to discuss. They were more concerned about getting treatment and pain relief at the end of their lives.

He hoped the debate could move on to a different level. 'What really matters is that the patient can make competent refusals of treatment. It gets us away from the much more difficult issue of termination of life, which is an issue which I think most patients don't want to contemplate at all.'

The younger hospital doctors raised other ethical concerns yesterday.

They said that they were expected to tell patients what their treatment would involve and what the consequences might be, so that the patient could give properly informed consent. But they found that what goes on in hospitals is far from satisfactory.

Paul Albert, doing his first year in hospital after medical school, said that although there were procedures for talking the patient through the treatment they were about to have, 'I have seen very few of these procedures performed and don't know enough of the details to get patients to give informed consent. A lot of patients are wheeled into theatre without really knowing what is about to happen to them. This is unsatisfactory. We are really sitting on a bit of a timebomb here.'

Dr Wilks agreed that procedures were not always followed, but argued against the setting up of a working party to put together guidelines for doctors. But the junior doctors' motion succeeded by a narrow margin on a card vote.

ADDITIONAL RESOURCES

You might like to contact the following organisations for further information. Due to the increasing cost of postage, many organisations cannot respond to enquiries unless they receive a stamped, addressed envelope.

Age Concern England
Education Department
Astral House
London, SW16 4ER
Tel: 0181 679 8000
Fax: 0181 765 7211
E-mail: ace@ace.org.uk
Age Concern information line provides a service to older people, their relatives, friends, carers and professionals. To obtain written information such as money, legal issues, health, community care and housing, telephone Freephone 0800 009966 open 7 days a week, 7am to 7pm

ALERT
27 Walpole Street
London, SW3 4QS
Tel: 0171 730 2800
Fax: 0171 730 1710
E-mail: alert@donoharm.co.uk
ALERT opposes euthanasia. They produce leaflets, a newsletter, booklets.

Alzheimer's Disease Society
Gordon House
10 Greencoat Place
London, SW1P 1PH
Tel: 0171 306 0606
Fax: 0171 306 0808
E-mail: info@alzheimers.org.uk
The Alzheimer's Disease Society produces a wide range of publications, 'What is Dementia' free fact sheet, for anyone who is interested in dementia. They also have a helpline (0845 300 0336 8am – 6pm Monday to Friday) offering advice and support.

British Humanist Association
47 Theobald's Road
London, WC1X 8SP
Tel: 0171 430 0908
Fax: 0171 430 1271
E-mail: robert@humanist.org.uk
Publishes a wide range of free briefings including the issues of racism, discrimination and prejudice, abortion, euthanasia and surrogacy.

British Medical Association (BMA)
BMA House
Tavistock Square
London, WC1H 9JP
Tel: 0171 387 4499
Fax: 0171 383 6400
E-mail: bma.org.uk
The BMA Tobacco Campaign was launched in 1984 to call for changes in Government policy on tobacco control. The BMA lobbies and advises politicians on a number of smoking issues and launches regular media campaigns. Please note that the BMA does not have the resources to deal with individual enquiries. However, they will respond to teacher's enquiries.

CARE Christian Action Research and Education
53 Romney Street
London, SW1P 3RF
Tel: 0171 233 0455
Fax: 0171 233 0983
A Christian charity which produces a wide range of publications presenting a Christian perspective on moral issues. Ask for their Resources Catalogue.

Centre for Bioethics and Public Policy
58 Hanover Gardens
London, SE11 5TN
Tel: 0171 587 0595
Fax: 0171 587 0595
E-mail: 100524.1567@compuserve.com
Opposes euthanasia

International Anti-Euthanasia Task Force (IAETF)
PO Box 760
Steubenville
OH43952
USA
Tel: 001 740 282 3810
Fax: 001 740 282 0769
E-mail: info@iaetf.org

Society for the Protection of Unborn Children (SPUC)
Phyllis Bowman House
5/6 St Matthew Street
London, SW1P 2JT
Tel: 0171 222 5845
Fax: 0171 222 0630
E-mail: enquiry@spuc.org.uk

The Christian Institute
26 Jesmond Road
Newcastle Upon Tyne, NE2 4PQ
Tel: 0191 281 5664
Fax: 0191 281 4272
E-mail: info@christian.org.uk
The Christian Institute is a non-denominational Christian organisation, concerned with the family, education and pro life issues and religious liberties.

Voluntary Euthanasia Society (EXIT)
13 Prince of Wales Terrace
London, W8 5PG
Tel: 0171 937 7770
Fax: 0171 376 2658
E-mail: ves.london@dial.pipex.com
The Society's principal aim is to make it legal for an adult person, who is suffering severe distress from an incurable illness, to receive medical help to die at their own considered request. The Society produces a range of publications including a student information pack, books a video tape and newsletters.

Voluntary Euthanasia Society – Scotland
17 Hart Street
Edinburgh, EH1 3RN
Tel: 0131 556 4404
Fax: 0131 557 4403
E-mail: didmsnj@easynet.co.uk
To make dying with dignity an option available to anyone, to protect patients and doctors alike in upholding the humanity of dying well, to seek legal reform, where necessary, and to introduce safeguards regarding voluntary euthanasia.

INDEX

* * * * *

Age Concern England
http://www.ace.org.uk
Age Concern England's web site has factsheets covering the following subject areas: income, legal issues, health, community care and housing. The site provides details about their library service, statistics about older people, their publications, reading lists and a frequently asked questions (FAQs) section. Well worth a visit.

Voluntary Euthanasia Society – Scotland
http://www.euthanasia.org
A huge site with sections on the following: Aims / beliefs / achievements, euthanasia (FAQ), self-deliverance, living wills, euthanasia in Holland, Australia, USA, etc., case histories, bibliography student research, VESS books, religion. There is also an On-line Webguide with links to other relevant sites.

Christian Medical Fellowship (CMF)
http://www.cmf.org.uk
A useful web site which offers a Christian perspective on euthanasia. Sections include: Euthanasia Twelve reasons why voluntary euthanasia should not be legalised, Submission from CMF to the select committee of the House of Lords on medical ethics, Euthanasia update, The Christian Case Against Euthanasia, Abortion and Euthanasia (Part 1), Abortion and Euthanasia (Part 2).

Voluntary Euthanasia Society (VES)
http://www.ves.org.uk
VES has a wide range of factsheets on its web site including the following: the case for euthanasia, objections, public opinion, medical opinion, the law, religion, views around the world, definitions and living wills. Their News section carries updates on the latest news relevant to the VES campaign, together with press releases and media briefings. News is organised with the most recent update first: although UK news is given in the most detail, they do try to give at least an overview of recent events world-wide. For more details on news from abroad, there are links to other sites around the world.

CARE Christian Action Research and Education
http://www.care.org.uk
This site offers a Christian perspective on Euthanasia. See the section: Euthanasia – Killing for Mercy? – A briefing paper about the issue.

Euthanasia.Com
http://www.euthanasia.com
A US based site which is committed to the fundamental belief that the direct killing of another person is wrong. The site has information on euthanasia, physician-assisted suicide, living wills, and mercy killing. A huge site.

ACKNOWLEDGEMENTS

The publisher is grateful for permission to reproduce the following material.

While every care has been taken to trace and acknowledge copyright, the publisher tenders its apology for any accidental infringement or where copyright has proved untraceable. The publisher would be pleased to come to a suitable arrangement in any such case with the rightful owner.

Chapter One: The Moral Debate

Frequently asked questions, © Chris Docker/The Voluntary Euthanasia Society of Scotland (VESS), *Answers to frequently asked questions*, © International Anti-Euthanasia Task Force (IAETF), 1998, *Public attitudes to voluntary euthanasia*, © D. Donnison and C. Bryson 'Matters of life and death: attitudes to euthanasia' in R. Jowell et al (eds) *British Social Attitudes the 13th Report*, Aldershot: Dartmouth, 1996, *Killing for mercy?*, © CARE, 1997, *Euthanasia – is it right?*, © EVA Magazine, June 1998, *The arguments for and against voluntary euthanasia*, © The Daily Record, June 1998, *There is a powerful case for legalising assisted dying*, © Voluntary Euthanasia Society, 1998, *The case against euthanasia*, © The Society for the Protection of Unborn Children (SPUC), *The debate that refuses to die*, © The Northern Echo, November 1998, *Public support will change the law*, © Voluntary Euthanasia Society, 1998, *Why my father had to die*, © The Independent on Sunday, December 1998, *Cast-iron argument for not giving up*, © East Anglian Daily Times, June 1998, *Lords warned over following Dutch road to euthanasia*, © Telegraph Group Limited, London 1998, *Freed, the woman who helped her sick mother to die*, © The Daily Mail, June 1998, *The will to live*, © Telegraph Group Limited, London 1998, *Attitudes to euthanasia*, © D. Donnison and C. Bryson 'Matters of life and death: attitudes to euthanasia' in R. Jowell et al (eds) *British Social Attitudes the 13th Report*, Aldershot: Dartmouth, 1996.

Chapter Two: The Medical Debate

What GPs really think about hastening death, © Pulse, November 1998, *Medical opinion*, © Voluntary Euthanasia Society, 1998, *Helping hand?*, © BMA News Review, September 1998, *Public attitudes to non-voluntary euthanasia*, © D. Donnison and C. Bryson 'Matters of life and death: attitudes to euthanasia' in R. Jowell et al (eds) *British Social Attitudes the 13th Report*, Aldershot: Dartmouth, 1996, *Euthanasia – should we let courts decide?*, © The Catholic Times, November 1998, *Kill or cure is not a choice for doctors*, © Telegraph Group Limited, London 1998, *Doctor, will you help me die?*, © Times Newspapers Limited, London 1998, *Psychiatrists' attitudes*, © The Lancet, October 1998, *Fighting to die with dignity*, © The Nursing Times, November 1998, *Dutch carry card that says: Don't kill me, doctor*, © Telegraph Group Limited, London 1998, *BMA moves on suicide*, © The Guardian, July 1998.

Photographs and illustrations:

Pages 1, 2, 21, 29, 33: Katherine Fleming, pages 3, 4, 8, 10, 11, 15, 16, 35, 36, 38, 39: Simon Kneebone, pages 7, 12, 23, 25, 27, 30, 32: Pumpkin House, pages 14, 19: Andrew Smith.

Craig Donnellan
Cambridge
April, 1999